YORK NOTES

A STREETCAR NAMED DESIRE

TENNESSEE WILLIAMS

NOTES BY HANA SAMBROOK
REVISED BY STEVE EDDY

PEARSON

YORK PRESS

YORK PRESS
322 Old Brompton Road, London SW5 9JH

PEARSON EDUCATION LIMITED
Edinburgh Gate, Harlow,
Essex CM20 2JE, United Kingdom
Associated companies, branches and representatives throughout the world

First published 1998
New edition 2003
This new and fully revised edition 2015

10 9 8

ISBN 978–1–4479–8226–5

Illustration on page 41 by Alan Batley
Phototypeset by Carnegie Book Production
Printed in China by Golden Cup

CONTENTS

PART FIVE: CONTEXTS AND INTERPRETATIONS

PART SIX: PROGRESS BOOSTER

PART SEVEN: FURTHER STUDY AND ANSWERS

HOW TO STUDY *A STREETCAR NAMED DESIRE*

These York Notes can be used in a range of ways to help you read, study and revise for your exam or assessment.

Become an informed and independent reader

Throughout the Notes, you will find the following key features to aid your study:

- **'Key context'** margin features: widen your knowledge of the setting, whether historical, social or political. This is highlighted by the AO3 (Assessment Objective 3) symbol to remind you of its connection to aspects you may want to refer to in your exam responses.
- **'Key interpretation'** boxes (a key part of AO5): do you agree with the perspective or idea that is explained here? Does it help you form your own view on events or characters? Developing your own interpretations is a key element of higher-level achievement in A Level, so make use of this and similar features.
- **'Key connection'** features (linked to AO4): whether or not you refer to such connections in your exam writing, having a wider understanding of how the play, or aspects of it, links to other texts or ideas can give you new perspectives on the text.
- **'Study focus'** panels: these help to secure your own understanding of key elements of the text. Being able to write in depth on a particular point or explain a specific feature will help your writing sound professional and informed.
- **'Key quotation'** features: these identify the effect of specific language choices – you could use these for revision purposes at a later date.
- **'Progress booster'** features: these offer specific advice about how to tackle a particular aspect of your study, or an idea you might want to consider discussing in your exam responses.
- **'Extract analysis'** sections: these are vital for you to use either during your reading or when you come back to the text afterwards. These sections take a core extract from a scene and explore it in real depth, explaining its significance and impact, raising questions and offering interpretations.

Stay on track with your study and revision

Your first port of call will always be your teacher, and you should already have a good sense of how well you are doing, but the Notes offer you several ways of measuring your progress.

- **'Revision task'**: throughout the Notes, there are some challenging, but achievable, written tasks for you to do relevant to the section just covered. Suggested answers are supplied in **Part Seven**.
- **'Progress check'**: this feature comes at the end of **Parts Two** to **Five**, and contains a range of short and longer tasks which address key aspects of the Part of the Notes you have just read. Below this is a grid of key skills which you can complete to track your progress, and rate your understanding.
- **'Practice task'** and **'Mark scheme'**: use these features to make a judgement on how well you know the text and how well you can apply the skills you have learned.

The edition used in these Notes is the Penguin Modern Classics edition, 2009.

A02 PROGRESS BOOSTER

You can choose to use the Notes as you wish, but as you read the play it can be useful to read over the Part Two summaries and analysis in order to internalise key events, ideas and developments in the plot.

A02 PROGRESS BOOSTER

Don't forget to make full use of Parts Three to Five of the Notes during your reading of the play. You may have essays to complete on **genre**, or key themes, or on the impact of specific settings, and can therefore make use of these in-depth sections. Or you may simply want to check out a particular idea or area as you're reading or studying the play in class.

A01 PROGRESS BOOSTER

Part Six: Progress Booster will introduce you to different styles of question and how to tackle them; help you to improve your expression so that it has a suitably academic and professional tone; assist you with planning and use of evidence to support ideas; and, most importantly, show you three sample exam responses at different levels with helpful AO-related annotations and follow-up comments. Dedicating time to working through this Part will be something you won't regret.

KEY CONTEXT A03

The clash between Stanley and Blanche is partly one between the declining 'aristocracy' of the South, which had never fully recovered economically from defeat in the Civil War (1861–5), and the up-and-coming working class. By the mid twentieth century, men like Stanley came back from the Second World War with a greater sense of entitlement to a share of the country's wealth. They were also empowered by the growth of trade unions.

KEY CONTEXT A03

The play is influenced by Williams's own life. His mother was a 'Southern belle' and his father an alcoholic travelling salesman. His sister Rose became increasingly unstable mentally and was eventually given a lobotomy. She spent the rest of her life in a mental institution. Williams reputedly felt guilty about his sister, and afraid of mental disintegration. He was also obsessed with death – like Blanche, who is haunted by the suicide of her husband.

A STREETCAR NAMED DESIRE: A SNAPSHOT

Why the play has stood the test of time

Tennessee Williams started to write *A Streetcar Named Desire* in 1945 – the year the war ended. It went through several versions before it was completed and first performed in 1947, with Stanley played by Marlon Brando. Brando also took the role, alongside Vivien Leigh as Blanche, in the 1951 film version. The play remains an intensely compelling one for modern audiences, because of its vivid characterisation, its masterfully developed conflicts and its enduring themes.

Powerful characterisation

Blanche DuBois is a complex, contradictory and endearing character – with all her faults. Stanley is a charismatic powerhouse whose smouldering sexuality and unquestioning self-confidence make him fascinating, despite his chauvinism and capacity for cruelty. Stanley's wife Stella, and his friend Mitch, lack the force of the two main characters, but perfectly complement their roles. Drama needs conflict, and the conflict between Stanley and Blanche builds steadily through the first ten scenes to its tragic resolution. Also important, however, are the inner conflicts: Stella must choose between her husband and her sister; Mitch is drawn to Blanche but cannot accept the reality of her past.

Gender and sexuality

Although the play is rooted in its time, the themes which emerge are timeless. One of these, as the title suggests, is sexual desire. Of course the play explores this in the context of post-war America. The sexual passion holding Stanley and Stella together is coloured by Stanley's belief that a man should be dominant, and by Stella's willingness to be dominated. Stanley's readiness to condemn Blanche's promiscuity, echoed by Mitch's disgust, is typical of the era. We may feel we have moved on as a society since 1947, but these gender issues, especially men's expectations of women, are still very much alive.

It has been suggested that in creating Blanche the playwright, who was homosexual, was indulging in imaginative cross-dressing, portraying a promiscuous heterosexual woman because homosexuality was then still illegal in most American states. However we view this possibility, we can appreciate that the play's title conveys his view of sexual passion as an unstoppable force that will take its victim along a path to self-destruction as surely as a streetcar.

Social class

Blanche is a 'Southern Belle' – a rather snobbish member of an old-established land-owning family, one of the 'plantation' families that originally got rich by using slave labour. Stella has for the most part been happy to abandon the family's standards in order to enjoy the animal passion she finds in Stanley, a proudly working-class man from a Polish immigrant family.

The American class system is different from the British, being based more on money and less on inherited status. These class issues still exist in modern Britain, albeit in different forms. Many people still attest to resentment and suspicion between classes, just as there is between Stanley and Blanche. In the play, these feelings drive the drama on.

Death, madness and tragedy

The plot lines of typical modern TV dramas reveal our continued fascination with death and violence. Death, after all, is the one thing humans can be sure of. We should therefore be able to relate easily to Blanche's obsession with death. Her decline into mental instability is in part the result of her experiences of death – her husband's suicide and her tending of dying relatives. Her breakdown in Scene Eleven can be seen as a kind of death, hinted at by her fantasy of dying at sea 'of eating an unwashed grape'. The play moves towards its tragic ending, leading us into an acceptance of this as inevitable. Blanche becomes a kind of sacrifice, reflecting the sacrificial origins of Greek **tragedy**.

Reading the play

Tennessee Williams wrote his plays for the stage, yet his **stage directions** often go far beyond practical instructions. Thus in the description of Elysian Fields at the start of Scene One, Williams speaks of the evening sky that *'gracefully attenuates the atmosphere of decay'*. When Blanche DuBois arrives on the scene, the description of her unsuitably dainty dress ends with the ominous words *'There is something about her uncertain manner … that suggests a moth'* (p. 3). These words hint at her helplessness, and **foreshadow** her tragic end. Yet the beauty of the language should not distract us from its meaning: the **metaphors** are a very accurate directive, hinting at what is to come.

Did Williams expect his plays to be read? Or is it simply that he found metaphors the most accurate means of conveying what he wanted to see on the stage? If you are reading the play and trying to envisage a stage performance, Williams's stage directions are beneficial in two ways: they help you to imagine the setting, certainly; in addition they offer you the pleasure of reading them, a pleasure that cannot be shared by theatre audiences.

 A04 **KEY CONNECTION**

Another playwright who wrote stage directions that went far beyond the need to instruct the director and actors was Williams's contemporary Arthur Miller, who wrote the introduction to the 2009 Penguin text of the play. Compare Williams's stage directions with those, for example, in Miller's *The Crucible* (Penguin, 2000).

 A04 **KEY CONNECTION**

The sexual tension between Blanche and Stanley, heightened by class differences, may bring to mind D. H. Lawrence's Lady Chatterley and the gamekeeper Mellors in the 1928 novel *Lady Chatterley's Lover*, or August Strindberg's Miss Julie and the footman Jean in the play *Miss Julie* (1888).

Study focus: Key issues to explore **A02**

As you study the text and revise, keep in mind these key elements and ideas:

- Blanche's role as a tragic figure whose downfall is inevitable
- How far Stella betrays her sister for sexual passion
- What motivates Stanley to destroy Blanche
- Whether there is ever any hope for a relationship between Blanche and Mitch
- How the main themes interconnect, especially desire, fate and death
- How Williams stage-manages tension, leading to the crisis of Scene Ten
- Williams's use of symbols, such as Blanche's baths, and lighting
- How Williams uses language, especially metaphor, in the stage directions
- How Williams uses music to signal and intensify action on stage

KEY CONTEXT

‘Belle Reve’, the name of the DuBois family mansion, means ‘beautiful dream’ in French. Louisiana was originally a French territory.

KEY CONNECTION

Williams makes use of a conventional theatrical device – the unseen eavesdropper – at the end of Scene Four. Shakespeare, for example, uses this in *Much Ado About Nothing*.

SYNOPSIS

Scenes One to Two

The play opens on a May evening in 1947, outside a shabby house in a rundown New Orleans street named Elysian Fields. The house belongs to Eunice and Steve Hubbel. Stanley and Stella Kowalski rent an apartment there.

Eunice is sitting on the steps with a black neighbour when the daintily dressed Blanche DuBois appears. She is Stella's older sister, arriving on a visit. She accepts Eunice's invitation to wait for Stella in the Kowalskis' apartment.

Stella returns and, though the sisters embrace affectionately, there is an underlying tension. Blanche is defensive, having sold the family property, Belle Reve, in circumstances that are never fully explained.

When Stanley comes home he accepts Blanche's presence, but it soon becomes obvious that her genteel pretensions will clash with his macho self-image. Through his questioning of Blanche we learn that she has been married and that her husband died.

The next evening (Scene Two) Stanley's friends Mitch, Steve and Pablo are coming to play poker, so Stella decides to take Blanche out for the evening. Stanley resents this arrangement. When Stella tells him of the 'loss' of Belle Reve, he suspects that Blanche has cheated Stella out of her share of the sale. As Stella's husband, he feels cheated too.

Stanley pulls out Blanche's trunk and accusingly displays the clothes and jewellery he thinks she has bought with the house sale money. Blanche comes in after a bath and her flirtatious manner makes him even more suspicious of her. He demands to see the bill of sale, explaining that he is anxious about his rights because Stella is expecting a baby.

Scenes Three to Six

Much later the same evening, the poker game is still in progress when the sisters return. Stanley has been drinking and he resents Blanche's interest in his shy bachelor friend Mitch.

There is a violent scene, with Stanley smashing the radio and hitting Stella. The hysterical Blanche takes her sister up to Eunice's flat, but is later shocked to find that Stella has gone back to Stanley.

The next day (Scene Four) Stella tells Blanche that she loves her husband and has no intention of leaving him. Stanley overhears Blanche's condemnation of him as an 'ape'.

Spurred on by resentment (Scene Five) Stanley makes enquiries about Blanche. He discovers that she was forced to leave Laurel, her home town, because of her reputation for promiscuity. His hints about her past terrify Blanche, and she tries to explain her behaviour to Stella, who encourages her hopes that she will marry Mitch. But even while waiting for Mitch, Blanche kisses a young subscription collector.

Blanche and Mitch return after an unsuccesful evening out (Scene Six). Mitch is painfully aware of his dullness. He comes in, and they converse awkwardly at first. Then Mitch talks about his sick mother, and Blanche about her husband's suicide after she found him with another man. Moved by her story, Mitch takes her in his arms. Suddenly Blanche is more hopeful.

Scenes Seven to Nine

It is now September, and Blanche's birthday. Stella has planned a dinner and invited Mitch. She is decorating a cake when Stanley enters triumphantly with details of Blanche's scandalous past. Stella refuses to believe these stories and is appalled to learn that Stanley has told Mitch. Blanche emerges from the bathroom in high spirits, but soon senses that something is wrong. Mitch does not arrive.

Scene Eight opens less than an hour later. The dismal dinner is over, and Blanche tries in vain to ring Mitch. She is growing increasingly frightened. Stanley has a birthday present for her – a bus ticket back to Laurel. Stella reproaches him for his cruelty, but stops abruptly when she goes into labour and has to go to the hospital.

Blanche has been drinking alone when Mitch arrives, unshaven and drunk (Scene Nine). Blanche is relieved to see him, but not for long. He accuses her of having lied to him about her age and her past. She admits her promiscuity but tries to explain it. Mitch is unsympathetic, and tries to have sex with her. Her wild cries of 'Fire!' frighten him off.

A03 **KEY CONTEXT**

Poker is a game of chance. As it involves concealing a poor hand by not showing any disappointment, it is traditionally thought of as a tough, masculine game. Characters in this play often conceal their emotions, or the facts.

Scenes Ten to Eleven

Alone again, Blanche goes on drinking steadily. Befuddled, and confused by her own fantasies, she dresses up in her tawdry finery while trying to pack her trunk.

Stanley arrives, a little drunk, from the hospital: the baby is not expected to arrive before morning. He mocks Blanche's claims that she is going on a cruise with a rich admirer and that Mitch returned penitent. Scared, Blanche breaks a bottle to defend herself, but Stanley easily disarms her and carries her off to the bedroom to rape her.

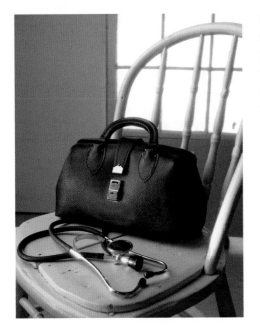

In Scene Eleven, several weeks have passed. Once more Stanley and his friends are playing poker. Blanche is heard offstage having a bath, while Stella packs her sister's trunk. Eunice enters and from her conversation with Stella we learn that Stella has arranged for Blanche to be taken to an asylum. Stella explains that she could not believe Blanche's story that Stanley raped her, and still go on living with him. Blanche believes that she is going on holiday with an old admirer.

A doctor and a matron from the asylum arrive. Blanche is frightened and tries to escape, but the matron restrains her. The doctor's courteous manner reassures her and she leaves on his arm. The sobbing Stella is given her child to hold and is soothed by Stanley's caresses.

KEY CONTEXT **A03**

In Greek mythology the Elysian Fields are the equivalent of paradise. There is irony in the choice of this name for a rundown street, but at the same time, the Elysian Fields were the dwelling-place of the dead. Blanche is obsessed with death.

KEY CONTEXT **A03**

The stage direction words '*suggests a moth*' hint at Blanche's fragility, and perhaps her preference for night-time. An earlier version of the play was entitled 'The Moth'.

SCENE ONE

Summary

- One evening in May 1947, Eunice is talking to a neighbour outside her home in the ironically named Elysian Fields, a shabby street in a poor district of New Orleans. Stanley Kowalski and Mitch arrive, on their way to go bowling. Stanley throws his wife Stella some meat.
- Blanche DuBois arrives, looking for her sister Stella's apartment. As Eunice and her husband Steve own the apartment, Eunice is able to let Blanche in.
- Blanche nervously helps herself to a drink while Eunice fetches Stella.
- When Stella arrives, the sisters embrace, but there is an undercurrent of tension. Blanche is critical of the apartment, then admits the loss of the family home, Belle Reve.
- Stanley greets Blanche pleasantly, but there is an uneasy atmosphere. Blanche tells him about the death of her husband some years ago.

Analysis

Blanche's shortcomings are revealed

The first scene introduces several important themes related to Blanche's weaknesses. Quite early on we discover her craving for drink. We also realise this does not go unnoticed by either her sister or her brother-in-law – his remark 'Liquor goes fast in hot weather' (p. 14) indicates this. In a play the point is stressed by repetitive action, while in a novel it might be made by the **authorial voice**.

We also see Blanche's awareness of social distinctions, which shows itself in the offhand manner in which she takes for granted both Eunice's and her neighbour's acts of kindness. To Blanche these are services to be expected of her social inferiors. Her attitude towards these two women prepares us for her condemnation of Stella's way of life, and, implicitly, of her husband.

Another aspect of her character revealed in this scene is her vanity and her need for flattery. There is **pathos** in this: Blanche is afraid of growing old and losing her looks, and needs flattery to banish her terrors. Appealing in her vulnerability, she is nevertheless very much the older sister, treating Stella as a child and expecting her to run errands.

Our attention is drawn immediately to Blanche – the greater part of the scene is devoted to building up her character by showing her actions and her reactions to the other characters (see Blanche in Characters and Themes).

First impressions of Stanley and Stella

Stanley also makes an impact: though we do not see much of him in this scene, Tennessee Williams sketches a portrait of him in stage directions that stress the sexual magnetism of this '*gaudy seed-bearer*' (p. 13), explaining Stella's infatuation. This sketch of Stanley's personality is, of course, withheld from the audience, who will rely on the actor to convey its full force.

But what of Stella herself? How much do we learn about her beyond what we learn from her words and actions? Her part in the play is significant, yet the introductory stage directions offer no description beyond '*a gentle young woman*' (p. 2). The audience will see the actress on the stage but the readers of the play must use their imagination and start to piece together a picture of Stella.

The significance of music in the play

Music is an aspect of the play that you cannot fully appreciate unless you see the play performed. An audience will hear the '*blue piano*' and the '*polka*' in Scene One, and repeatedly throughout the play. In the stage directions, Williams tells us that the blue piano symbolises this part of New Orleans, but its use as a dramatic device is not consistent.

By contrast, the second **motif**, the polka that only Blanche and the theatre audience can hear, has considerable dramatic weight; it recalls the last time Blanche danced with her husband Allan, moments before his suicide. The use of music to alert the audience to a significant fact (here the suicide and Blanche's guilty feelings about it) is unusual. This is especially true as it is used not only to create an atmosphere (as the blue piano does to some extent) but also to stress an important aspect of the plot and of Blanche's character. The stage directions offer no explanation, and both the audience and the reader will come to realise the significance of the polka only gradually, the whole story being told in Scene Six.

A03 **PROGRESS BOOSTER**

Readers have only Williams's descriptions of the music to guide them, yet perhaps the presence of stage directions stresses its importance more. The audience in a theatre, concentrating on the action, may not pay much attention to background music. After all, we are all used to music in films, and have perhaps learned to disregard it, though it may still affect our feelings about what we are watching. When reading the play, think about how your attention is drawn to the music through the stage directions.

A02

Study focus: Stage directions and characters' language

As a reader of the play, there is another way in which you will benefit from the stage directions. They are evocative, precise in their use of imagery, and inevitably contrast with the language used by most of the characters, with the exception of Blanche and Stella. The language of the stage directions underlines the uneducated speech of most of the characters. By contrast, Blanche's quotation from Edgar Allan Poe's poem 'Ulalume' reminds us that she is (or was) an English teacher and hints at her cultured background.

The stage directions also draw our attention to the two main characters of the play. Compare the descriptions of Blanche and Stanley. She is unsuitably dressed as if for a garden party, her white suit in some soft material, her fluttering manner suggesting a moth; he is described as a '*gaudy seed-bearer*', proudly aware of his masculinity. Again the stage directions offer help to the reader as much as to the director and cast.

Extract analysis: Scene One, pp. 11–12

This passage is taken from the introductory scene, from Stella's 'Stop this…' to her 'Does that surprise you?' It demonstrates Williams's skill in writing **dialogue** that adds to our understanding of the characters, and also to our store of information about earlier events that have built up the **dramatic tension** of the play. It begins during a heated exchange between Stella and Blanche. The two sisters have met, embraced and spoken lightly (and in Blanche's case a little condescendingly) about New Orleans, about the Kowalskis' humble apartment and about Stella's husband. Blanche has admitted to being unwell, and Stella has observed that she seems 'nervous or overwrought'.

The DuBois family mansion, Belle Reve, means a great deal to Blanche and Stella. Not surprisingly, then, in this scene Blanche is anxious about revealing its loss. She expects Stella to blame her, and readers (or the audience) may sense that she feels guilty and is forestalling possible criticism by accusing Stella before Stella can accuse her.

Stella tries to extract the plain facts of the matter from her sister, but Blanche refuses to cooperate. In a long speech, full of unspoken (but strongly hinted at) horrors of her life at Belle Reve she speaks of her own suffering and of her sister's selfish indifference. The speech is reproachful and wounding, and is meant to be: we might remember here the saying that attack is the best defence. The scene ends with Stella in tears, going off to wash her face.

Stella and Blanche are very different. The passage is just one page long, yet we learn a great deal from it about their differences. First, the two sisters are quite unlike one another in emotional make-up. Stella interrupts her sister's self-dramatising reproaches with a cutting comment on her 'hysterical outburst' and on her emotive phrase 'fought and bled'. Stella quotes Blanche's words deliberately; the repetition is perhaps intended to deflate Blanche's histrionics and lower the emotional temperature.

Blanche reacts at once by declaring that Stella's attitude was only to be expected. It seems likely that the confrontation follows a long-established pattern of rows between the sisters. Blanche's words 'The loss – the loss …' show that she still finds it difficult to speak of what has happened. She slowly comes to admit that Belle Reve has been sold, and Stella's reaction is as typical of her as Blanche's histrionics are of Blanche. She *'looks slowly down at her hands folded on the table'*, her silence expressing her distress. Williams pays great attention to detail in his stage directions, right down to the *'yellow-checked linoleum'*. Blanche makes a typically theatrical gesture as she *'touches her handkerchief to her forehead'* – she is reluctant to give any more information.

KEY CONTEXT   **A03**

'Belle Reve' means 'Beautiful Dream' in French, an echo of the time when Louisiana (named after King Louis XIV) was a French territory, before being sold to the United States by Napoleon in 1803. The name implies that the lifestyle of wealthy plantation owners like the DuBois family was elegant but, like all dreams, bound to come to an end. Their wealth was based on slavery, abolished in 1865, after the North won the Civil War. Blanche's 'I fought and bled' sounds like the **rhetoric** of the defeated South.

Stella wants to know the facts, but it becomes clear that Blanche cannot, or will not, provide them – and her confrontation with Stanley in Scene Two will reinforce this. This leaves it open to question whether her failure to give the details is due to her ignorance of business matters or to deliberate evasion. Blanche's words *'accusing me* of it!' are very revealing: as Stella has not spoken a word of reproach, we can only assume that Blanche's own guilty feelings are prompting her here. Later, in Scene Nine, we learn that she already indulged in wild behaviour while still living at Belle Reve, and it may well be that her drinking and her one-night stands contributed to her inability to cope with the sorry financial state of Belle Reve, as much as the expensive funerals.

Blanche's experiences have left her with much anxiety about death. In her long speech about the deaths at Belle Reve we notice her use of a **metaphor** of physical injury – *'I took the blows in my face and my body!'*– which echoes her earlier *'I fought and bled'*. The images of messy death, of blood and physical pain proliferate in her speech: 'the long parade to the graveyard'; Margaret so swollen with disease that she could not be fitted into a coffin and had to be burned like rubbish; the hoarse breathing, the death rattle of the dying, their desperate clinging to life – 'Don't let me go!'; the bleeding – later, in Scene Nine, Blanche tells Mitch of the 'blood-stained pillow-slips' (p. 88).

Blanche's account is all the more affecting for what is left unsaid. We might also notice here the absence of sentimentality, indeed of any emotional involvement, in her description of the deaths. Is this due to self-discipline, or to self-absorption and lack of empathy? She speaks jokingly of the 'Grim Reaper' who 'had put up his tent on our doorstep!' but the death scenes are stamped on her mind. Her experiences in her last years at Belle Reve clearly affected her already precarious mental balance. We may remember this later, in Scene Nine, when the symbolic figure of the Mexican seller of paper flowers for the dead brings to Blanche's mind 'a house where dying old women remembered their dead men' (p. 88).

Within this dramatic speech we (and Stella) find a few practical comments on the recurrent funeral expenses, not covered by insurance – except for Cousin Jessie's hundred dollars which just paid for her coffin, but not for her funeral. This sudden descent into practicalities is characteristic of Blanche: later, in Scene Two, after her melodramatic outburst when Stanley touches her dead husband's poems, she puts on her glasses to go methodically through a pile of mortgage documents.

Blanche's resentment of Stella's absence is obvious. She reminds her sister bitterly that she only came home for the funerals, which are quiet and 'pretty compared to deaths', with 'gorgeous' coffins and beautiful flowers. She reminds Stella of her 'pitiful salary' in an appeal for sympathy, tinged maybe with self-dramatisation. Some of Blanche's resentment is evidently due to sexual jealousy of her younger sister, who got away, found a husband and was 'In bed with [her] Polack' while her sister watched over deathbeds. This is a double insult: a hint at Stella's sexual appetite, and Blanche's contempt for an immigrant.

Though she remains silent while Blanche is attacking her, Stella will not tolerate insults to her husband: 'That's enough!' This **foreshadows** Stella's defence of Stanley in Scene Four. Blanche seems surprised when she realises that Stella is crying. Perhaps this is because Stella is usually firmly in control of herself; however, we may also guess that Blanche lacks insight into other people's feelings.

 KEY INTERPRETATION

The images of bleeding and death in Blanche's long speech are striking even in the context. We wonder about the image of her husband's violent death here: his memory seems to have conditioned Blanche to retain in her mind the grisly reality of dying.

 **KEY INTERPRETATION**

Blanche appears quite matter-of-fact about the deaths at Belle Reve. Is the lack of emotion in her memories of the dying a self-protective mechanism or an indication of her self-absorption?

SCENE TWO

Summary

- The sisters prepare to go out for supper, as Stanley and his friends will be playing poker in the apartment. Stanley is annoyed that Stella will not be home to serve him a hot meal.
- Stanley is furious at the loss of Belle Reve. He believes that under Louisiana law his wife's property also belongs to him, and that therefore he has been cheated.
- Stanley opens Blanche's trunk and displays her clothes and jewellery, which he believes to be expensive and bought with the house sale money. Stella is upset and runs out.
- Blanche comes in after a bath. She flirts with Stanley, but he refuses to compliment her.
- Stanley demands to see the papers relating to the sale of Belle Reve. Looking for them, he finds instead a sheaf of Blanche's love-letters from her dead husband.
- When Blanche hands Stanley a strongbox of papers he seems a little ashamed and explains that any inheritance would be important because Stella is expecting a baby.
- Stella comes in and the sisters embrace. As they set out, Stanley's friends arrive.

Analysis

Stanley's resentment and suspicion grow

In this scene Stanley's antagonism towards Blanche grows, as do his suspicions about her. Both the motive and the means for her destruction are now becoming clear, as the playwright prepares the ground for the inevitable tragedy.

From the beginning of the scene Stanley seems to resent the fact that Stella is taking Blanche out for supper. He asks, 'How about my supper, huh?' (p. 16). He may be annoyed that Stella is not going to serve him a hot meal, but there may also be a class element to his irritation, as Galatoires' is a high-class restaurant. Moreover, Stella will presumably pay the bill with money that Stanley has earned. On the other hand, she is largely going out because he will be taking over the apartment for the evening with his poker party. Is his attitude at all justified?

Class antagonism

Stanley's hostility to Blanche is rooted in the class differences between himself and Blanche (and by implication his wife as well). His instinctive reaction is to try to drag Blanche down to his own level, using his sexuality as a means of domination, as he appears to have done with Stella. Later on, in Scene Eight, he makes this instinct explicit, telling Stella: 'I pulled you down off them columns [of Belle Reve] and how you loved it' (p. 81).

This class antagonism is intensified by Stanley's suspicions that he has been cheated by the smart-talking Blanche. When he pulls out Blanche's clothes and jewellery he betrays his ignorance of their true value – they are less expensive than he thinks. Again he is at a loss and his resentment grows because his wife mocks him. She knows the true value of Blanche's possessions – for example, that rhinestone is 'Next door to glass' (p. 19), partly because she is a woman, but also because she comes from a wealthier background.

Key quotation: Stella's wilful ignorance   **A01**

On page 17, Stella tells Stanley: 'There weren't any papers, she didn't show any papers, I don't care about papers.'

Stella is referring to Blanche's failure to produce a bill of sale for Belle Reve. She was shocked to hear that the family home had been 'lost', as Blanche vaguely put it, but now she is prepared to accept this vagueness. Her repetition shows her exasperation with Stanley for wanting to know *how* it was lost.

Do you think Stella shows a lack of intelligence here, a lack of interest in material wealth, or a reluctance to question Blanche?

A03 KEY CONTEXT

Blanche, in her red robe, is posturing flirtatiously; surely there is a suggestion here of the scarlet woman (prostitute) of the Bible (Revelation 17). This signal may be picked up more easily on the printed page.

A03 KEY CONTEXT

In the Bible (Matthew 15:14), Jesus says 'And if the blind lead the blind, both shall fall into a ditch.' Blanche's use of the proverb seems to hint at impending disaster.

How the scene is structured

Williams has divided the scene into two parts: first we have Stella telling her husband how to treat the highly-strung visitor, and revealing the loss of Belle Reve. Already resentful at being told that he has to avoid upsetting Blanche, Stanley explodes in anger at being swindled, and grows angrier still when his wife laughs at him for overestimating the value of Blanche's wardrobe.

The second part of the scene begins after Stella rushes off, with Blanche making an appearance in her red robe. Blind to Stanley's rage she postures flirtatiously. Her manner arouses Stanley's suspicions in another direction. He is experienced and shrewd enough to sense that his sister-in-law's provocative behaviour is more fitting for a prostitute than a schoolteacher: 'If I didn't know that you was my wife's sister I'd get ideas about you!' (p. 22).

The main function of the scene is to set the tragedy in motion. A theatre audience would easily pick up the warning signals, especially in the second half of the scene, with Stanley's smouldering rage set against Blanche's dangerously misguided playfulness. Readers of the play are guided by Williams's stage directions and the text of the dialogues – and their own imagination.

Frightening ambiguities

There are ambiguities in this scene: why is Blanche frightened by the tamale vendor's cry 'Red hots! Red hots!' (p. 25)? And what does she mean by the reference to the Gospels, 'The blind are – leading the blind!' (p. 26)? In the theatre the menacing atmosphere created by this first conflict between Blanche and Stanley will ensure that the audience accept Blanche's despairing cry unquestioningly. When reading the play, we will still identify Blanche's terror and accept the approach of a catastrophe – even if we cannot arrive at a clear interpretation of the last part of this scene.

Study focus: Symbolic motifs

Note that a new **motif** is introduced in this scene and will recur again and again: Blanche's passion for taking long baths. On a purely practical level, this habit is obviously very irritating to the other occupants of the apartment and will increase the tension significantly. The apartment only has one bathroom (presumably unlike Belle Reve), and the apartment is so small that it gets steamed up when Blanche finally opens the door. As so often with Williams, however, there is a symbolic aspect to this obsessive habit. It represents Blanche's yearning to wash away the guilt for her husband's death, and of her many sexual encounters. If the motif strikes us as repetitive and intrusive, it should be remembered that in the continuing action of the play a theatre audience would probably not notice it so much. By contrast, the blue piano, which can stand for the spirit of the French quarter of New Orleans or more generally for vitality and pleasure, can also signal a change to a lower key in the mood of the scene. Providing a musical background with no specific message, it remains neutral: *the perpetual "blue piano"*.

Revision task 1: Character tensions

Make notes on the main sources of tension between characters that you have identified so far, and which could ultimately lead to tragedy.

You could consider:

- Social class differences
- Blanche's life at Belle Reve
- Stanley's suspicions
- Blanche's behaviour

SCENE THREE

Summary

- Late the same night the men are still playing poker. The sisters return and Stanley snubs Blanche for her genteel airs. She is drawn to Mitch, a shy bachelor.
- Stanley orders the sisters to be quiet and turns off Blanche's radio. She turns it on again and Stanley throws it out of the window. Stella rushes at him, and he hits her.
- Stanley's friends restrain and calm him, but Blanche runs in hysterically to collect Stella's clothes. Both sisters go upstairs to sleep in Eunice's apartment.
- Stanley sobers up and shouts for Stella. She appears and they embrace passionately. Blanche is appalled to find that her sister has gone back to her husband.
- Mitch reassures Blanche that the Kowalskis are 'crazy about each other' (p. 38).

Analysis

A clash of male and female worlds

In this scene, notice the division into the competitive male world of the poker game, and the female world in which relationships seem more important than competition. The stage directions deserve our attention for their vivid description of the poker game. Notice especially Williams's reference to a Van Gogh painting of a similar scene. This underlines the significance of the visual elements, of light and of hard primary colours, linking them to the men's harsh masculinity.

The poker party's dramatic purpose is to demonstrate Stanley's domination of his friends: he makes all the decisions in their game. The scene shows their devotion to him through their tender handling of him when he is drunk.

The sequence of cause and effect may be traced also in Stanley's drunken rage when he hits Stella. Her returning to him that same night is further proof of the strength of her passion, in which his violent behaviour is part of the attraction. Blanche's hysterical determination to take Stella away from Stanley (which continues into Scene Four) is not forgotten or forgiven by Stanley. It makes him all the more determined to be rid of her. The animosity between the two, with its sexual undertones brought into play by Blanche's flirtatious behaviour, foreshadows the shocking climax that will destroy Blanche's sanity.

A02 **PROGRESS BOOSTER**

The relationship between Mitch and Stanley is particularly important for the plot. That Stanley is jealous of Mitch's interest in Blanche is made clear by his calling Mitch back to the poker game. Moreover, he is watching Mitch: 'He was looking through them drapes' (p. 32) – at Blanche.

Blanche's contradictory character

In this scene we also learn more about Blanche: her vanity betrays her into the foolish lie about Stella's age, and into the equally foolish claim that she has come in order to help out as her sister has not been well. We also notice curious inconsistencies in her behaviour. Blanche's seductive posturing, half-undressed, in the gap between the curtains to the bedroom, will be remembered when Stanley reveals her promiscuous past (Scene Seven). To her such behaviour is instinctive when there are men around. Her behaviour underlines the contradictions in her character. Williams presents her as both the genteel Southern lady who expects men to stand up when she enters, and who cannot bear a rude remark or a vulgar action – and a cheap seductress.

Another aspect of Blanche's character is shown by the purchase of a Chinese lantern to put over the light bulb. It will play a part in Mitch's disillusionment with her in Scene Nine, but it may also be seen as a symbol of Blanche's refusal to face the ugly reality of her life.

Study focus: Blanche's neediness

Bear in mind that for the play to work as a tragedy, Williams needs to make us sympathise with Blanche. In this scene, her attempts to attract Mitch show her neediness. Her conversation with him at the close of the scene emphasises the class differences between them, and draws our attention to his efforts to overcome them. The artificiality of Blanche's words stresses her awareness of the cultural gap between them and her desperate determination to attract Mitch despite this gap.

Key quotation: Blanche's vulnerability **A01**

Blanche tells Mitch 'I need kindness now' (p. 39).

It is perhaps telling that, although she has only just met Mitch, Blanche does seem to be genuinely confiding in him here. Has she been shocked into it by the unexpected violence with which the poker party broke up? These words, moving in their honesty, will be echoed in the last scene when she says to the doctor: 'I have always depended on the kindness of strangers' (p. 107). The words are the author's appeal on Blanche's behalf for the audience to understand and pity her.

SCENE FOUR

Summary

- The morning after the poker party, Stella is still in bed, alone but happy. Blanche rushes in, hysterical after a sleepless night. She reproaches Stella for going back to her husband and sleeping with him.

- Stella explains that Stanley is always violent when drunk and that he is now ashamed of himself. Her calm acceptance outrages Blanche, who wants to take Stella away from the situation. She listens in disbelief when Stella tells her that she has no intention of leaving Stanley.

- Stanley's violent behaviour is related to his dominance and powerfulness, a large part of his sexual attraction for his wife. Yet Blanche condemns Stanley as a savage, a 'survivor of the Stone Age' (p. 47), bringing home the raw meat (remember Stanley's blood-stained parcel of meat in Scene One).

- While Blanche condemns Stanley, he approaches unseen and hears it all. He withdraws and returns noisily, calling for Stella. They embrace and Stanley grins triumphantly at Blanche over Stella's head.

Analysis

The sisters' different attitudes to sexual relationships

It becomes clear that the sisters have very different attitudes to the violent scene the night before. The opening stage directions contrast Stella's sleepy sensuality with her sister's hysteria. Stella is reading '*a book of coloured comics*' (p. 40), a silent reminder that she has accepted Stanley's values and joined a world in which comics, not books, are read. Though this scene seems at first to provide an interval of calm, the tensions quickly build up. Blanche fails to understand Stella's passionate marriage. It seems that Blanche, despite all her sexual experience (about which we learn in Scene Seven), has never experienced true passion.

Below the surface the sisters do understand one another; they both know that they are speaking of sexual passion. Yet while Stella's passion for her husband endures, Blanche's affairs have been brief, lasting only 'when the devil is in [her]' (p. 46). Stella has no patience with Blanche's hysterical plans, and her irritation shows in her **ironic** comments. She starts to resent her sister's disapproval and harsh criticism of Stanley. Will this play a part in her decision in the last scene?

Study focus: The symbol of the streetcar

Be aware of the symbolic importance of what Blanche calls the 'rattle-trap streetcar' of desire (p. 46). Stella asks bluntly if Blanche has ever ridden on it. Blanche's reply, 'It brought me here', can mean simply that the streetcar to Desire (a real district of New Orleans) brought her to her sister's house, but equally it is a **metaphor** for the sexual desire that has ruined her life and brought her to New Orleans to live on her sister's charity. In Scene One Blanche says that she transferred from the 'streetcar named Desire' to one called 'Cemeteries' (p. 3). What does this suggest about the relationship between desire and death?

A03 **KEY CONTEXT**

Tennessee Williams had actually seen in New Orleans a streetcar with the curious destination 'Desire'. Apart from being the title of the play, the streetcar is mentioned in Scenes One and Four.

Dramatic structure

The scene has a dramatic function, as well as telling us more about the sisters. When Stanley overhears Blanche's melodramatic condemnation of him as an ape-man, he has even more reason to dislike her and want to be rid of her. His triumphant grin at the close of the scene promises ill for Blanche.

Stanley's overhearing Blanche's condemnation of him (a time-honoured dramatic device) strengthens his dislike of her and gives him good reason – in his view – to try to get rid of her.

Additionally, Blanche's hysteria (for instance, in her attempt to phone her old admirer Shep) casts doubt on her sanity. This again is sure to influence Stella's readiness to have her sister committed to a mental hospital.

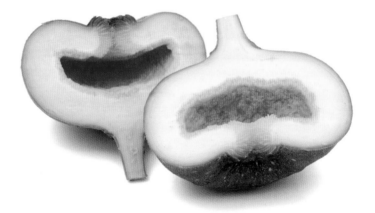

Revision task 2: Stella and Blanche

Make a table comparing what you know about Stella and Blanche so far. Include:

- Their attitudes towards men
- Their attitudes towards violence
- How cultured they appear to be
- Their attitude towards social class
- How contented each woman is

Include short relevant quotations to back up your points.

SCENE FIVE

Summary

- A noisy row is heard from upstairs as Eunice accuses Steve of infidelity. She rushes out, with Steve following, while the sisters listen below, amused.

- Stanley returns from bowling. It is clear from Blanche's nervous behaviour that she is afraid of him. He tells her that an acquaintance of his met her at a disreputable hotel in Laurel, the town where she taught. Blanche denies this but looks terrified.

- When Stanley leaves, Blanche tries to find out what her sister knows about her past, and tries to explain her past behaviour. She admits that she is nervous: Mitch is coming to take her out on a date, and she is desperate to attract him. She is afraid of growing old alone.

- Stella tries to reassure her as she leaves to join Stanley. She encourages Blanche's hopes of marrying Mitch.

- A young man calls, collecting subscriptions to a paper. Blanche flirts with him and kisses him, then sends him on his way, just before Mitch's arrival.

Analysis

Blanche confides in Stella

A threatening undertone runs through this scene. It opens with a violent row between Eunice and Steve, which is followed by a hostile exchange between Stanley and Blanche. It is clear that Stanley has discovered something about Blanche's past and that she is frightened.

Blanche speaks hesitantly to Stella about her attempts to gain the protection of men friends. Her description of her efforts to attract and keep men, dressing in the soft colours of butterfly wings, recalls her moth-like first appearance in Elysian Fields. We are reminded of her fragility and vulnerability, and of her fear of losing her beauty. She is aware that she is growing older and feels she must prevent men from seeing this. Her use of the **metaphor** of the paper lantern refers back to her conversation with Mitch in Scene Three – 'I can't stand a naked light-bulb' (p. 34). It also anticipates Mitch's contemptuous tearing-off of the Chinese lantern in Scene Nine – an action repeated by Stanley in Scene Eleven.

Blanche's confession to Stella about her fears for the future and her hopes of finding safety with Mitch is harrowing because she now admits, however indirectly, her past liaisons and recognises that they were just a way of asserting her existence.

A05 **KEY INTERPRETATION**

Stanley's refusal to kiss Stella in front of Blanche could show that he is inhibited in Blanche's presence, or that he resents his wife for allowing her to stay with them.

A03 **KEY CONTEXT**

Blanche calls Mitch 'my Rosenkavalier!' Literally 'the knight of the rose', Rosenkavalier is the hero of Strauss's comic-romantic opera by the same name (1911). This hints at Blanche's culture and liking for fantasy.

KEY INTERPRETATION

The episode with the young subscription collector could be an illustration of Blanche's reckless character, or a dramatic device necessary to the plot.

PROGRESS BOOSTER

Remember that in a tragedy the playwright has to create a sense of inevitable downfall. Dramatically this episode does more than make us doubt Blanche's real desires. For most readers – or audience members – there is now little possibility of a happy ending for her, given the set of circumstances that have been established in the play so far. The questions now remain only when and how Blanche's final downfall will come about.

A sense of foreboding grows

There is a sense of foreboding in this scene as Blanche cries over the stain on her white shirt – is it a symbol of lost innocence or a reminder of her husband's tragic end? We become aware of the inevitability of disaster because Blanche's past suggests that she will always go astray, propelled by sexual desire as well as by an instinctive rejection of the dull security she professes to need. The point is driven home by her flirtation with the young man collecting for a local newspaper, and particularly by what she says to him. The innuendo of 'You make my mouth water' (p. 57) and the open confession of past misdeeds in 'keep my hands off children' (p. 57) strongly hints at what kind of scandal put an end to Blanche's teaching career and drove her away from Laurel. The throbbing of the blue music and the distant thunder in the last part of this scene perhaps speak of sexual passion too.

Study focus: Blanche's self-destructive nature

How do you interpret the brief episode with the young man? Certainly Williams uses it to show the contradictions in Blanche's character. She is desperate to marry Mitch, yet she is ready to risk her future in this flirtatious moment. Is it an urge to self-destruct? Does she really find this young man (or handsome young men in general) so irresistible? Or is it that she has no real desire for the safety of married life because in her heart she cannot commit herself to a permanent relationship with one man – like a moth that will flutter and not settle down? Williams clearly intends to arouse questions about why Blanche puts at risk the material and emotional security she desires. There is plenty of room here for you to offer an informed personal interpretation, backed up by evidence from the text.

Key quotation: Blanche begins to confide in Stella

Blanche comes close to admitting the truth of her behaviour in Laurel when she tells Stella: 'I've run for protection, Stella, from under one leaky roof to another leaky roof' (p. 53).

At this point in the play, Stanley has just confronted Blanche with the information that he knows a man named Shaw who claims he met Blanche at the disreputable Hotel Flamingo in Laurel. Blanche has denied this, but perhaps now she feels she has to prepare Stella for the awful truth emerging. Typically, she uses the euphemistic **metaphor** of the 'leaky roof' for men who offer her a very limited security in return for love-making. Stella seems to ignore Blanche's attempt at honesty. Is she being insensitive, or refusing even to consider the truth behind what Blanche is saying?

SCENE SIX

Summary

- It is after midnight when Mitch and Blanche return. The evening has not been a success, and Mitch feels he has been dull. Blanche invites him in for a drink.
- At first the conversation remains awkward in spite of Blanche's feverish attempts at gaiety. It seems that the best Mitch can manage is to talk about his weight.
- Blanche tells Mitch that Stanley does all he can to offend her. Mitch is sympathetic.
- When Mitch asks Blanche her age, she avoids answering by asking why he wants to know. When he says his mother asked, this leads to a more serious discussion, with Mitch talking about his ailing mother, and Blanche of the suicide of her husband after she found him in bed with another man.
- Mitch, deeply moved, embraces Blanche as she weeps.

Analysis

Blanche's efforts to lighten the mood

The opening mood of this scene is downbeat and depressing; the evening out has been a failure, and both Mitch and Blanche know it. While Mitch apologises for his dullness, Blanche's reaction is to make a desperate attempt to be light-hearted. She pretends to the baffled Mitch that they are in a bohemian café in Paris. Her attempt is of course doomed to failure. This highlights her inability to understand other people, isolated as she is in the world of her imagination.

Blanche's inability to face reality

Blanche's play-acting is a prelude to a dramatic change of mood when she and Mitch talk seriously. It has another purpose as well: to stress her need for make-believe situations which make her blighted life bearable. Indeed Blanche is almost incapable of facing reality – not only its uglier aspects, but its humdrum ordinary demands as well. She sees Mitch as her salvation, but could she bear the life of the wife of a factory worker?

One reality that Blanche successfully avoids in this scene is her age. Mitch's asking how old she is could be seen as ungentlemanly, and she could refuse to tell him on these grounds, but it makes Blanche nervous – for the obvious reason that she is older than he probably thinks. It may be that she is at first just being evasive when she asks him why he wants to know, and then why he spoke to his mother about her, but she does seem to sympathise and be moved by his sensitivity when he shows how much he loves his mother and fears her imminent death. This also leads Blanche to confide in him far more deeply than we might have expected at the start of the scene. She tells him about her young husband's suicide. Dramatically, this has the function of telling the audience about it in detail too, and gaining more of our sympathy at a point when we must be starting to feel that her survival is threatened.

A03   **KEY CONTEXT**

Blanche refers to the novel *La Dame aux camélias* (1848) by Alexandre Dumas the Younger. Its heroine is a high-class Parisian call girl. The association is continued with the words '*Voulez-vous coucher avec moi ce soir?*' (p. 61), the standard invitation of a French prostitute to a passing man.

A02

Progress booster: Blanche's contradictions

It's important that you can write about how Blanche sometimes seems to risk losing what at other times she seems to want. There are moments in this scene that hint at her unwillingness to go on with the pretence necessary in her relationship with Mitch. While pretending to be in a Paris café she bluntly offers to sleep with him – but in French, certain that he will not understand. Again, when speaking of her old-fashioned ideas about how a gentleman should behave, she rolls her eyes self-mockingly, knowing that he cannot see her face. On both these occasions she risks being found out by Mitch. As in the episode with the young man in the preceding scene she recklessly endangers her hard-won position with Mitch, as if in her heart she wishes to avoid the dull safety of marriage. And yet at the close of the scene her humble gratitude is sincere. It puzzles us yet engages our sympathy; Blanche is a complex, contradictory character and that makes her successful as a focus for the drama.

KEY CONNECTION A04

What Blanche begins to identify as 'the hostility of [sexual attraction]' is also present in *The Duchess of Malfi*, in Ferdinand's incestuous feelings towards the Duchess.

Blanche begins to understand Stanley

In this scene we witness Blanche's half-formed speculations about why Stanley dislikes her: 'there is such a thing as the hostility of –' (p. 65). She suggests that Stanley's dislike of her might be fuelled by sexual attraction. Her knowledge of men, gained in all those one-night stands in Laurel, is obvious here though never comprehended by the simple Mitch. Do you think it strange that Blanche has apparently not worked out this possible reason for the tension between her and Stanley before?

As well as casting light on her past, her speculation foreshadows her devastating encounter with Stanley in Scene Ten. The rape that will drive her into her fantasy world for good is foretold here and its motive defined accurately, as will be acknowledged by Stanley in the later scene – 'We've had this date with each other from the beginning!' (p. 97). The dramatic device of forewarning the audience or readers of what is going to happen is used here only indirectly. It might pass unnoticed in a stage performance, but it will be clearer to you, reading the printed text.

Study focus: Musical motifs

A02

Notice Williams's stage directions relating to music. The low-key mood of this scene is underlined by the absence of the blue piano. The polka music, on the other hand, plays an important part in Blanche's revelations about her husband's suicide and the reasons for it. The polka has been heard before as an indirect reference to Blanche's past (Scene One), but only now do we realise its full meaning. In order for the music to be dramatically effective, we must remember that Blanche alone (along with the audience) can hear it, together with the gunshot that always brings it to an end.

A05 KEY INTERPRETATION

It could be that Blanche still feels such guilt at not being able to 'save' her husband from his homosexuality, and for his death, that she cannot believe she deserves love.

Key quotation: Blanche dares to hope

A02

At the end of the scene, when Mitch embraces Blanche, she is suddenly hopeful, exclaiming, 'Sometimes – there's God – so quickly!' (p. 68).

This is typical of the dramatic lines with which several of the scenes end. It comes as a sudden outpouring of emotion from Blanche, mixed with hope and perhaps gratitude. She has confided in Mitch, and it seems that her honesty has been rewarded. The reference to God is not characteristic of Blanche: she takes comfort in men, not religion. The wording suggests that most of the time God does not really exist for her, but at a time like this it seems her prayer has been answered.

Revision task 3: Blanche and Mitch

A02

Make notes on the key moments in the development of the relationship between Blanche and Mitch so far, with key quotations to represent them.

Now, looking at your notes, how much do you think Williams want us to believe that Blanche could marry Mitch and live 'happily ever after'?

SCENE SEVEN

Summary

- It is now September, and Blanche's birthday. While Blanche has a bath, Stella decorates the birthday cake.
- Stanley enters triumphantly with details of Blanche's past: she was promiscuous even while living at Belle Reve, meeting drunken soldiers at night. After the house sale she moved to a cheap, disreputable hotel, but even here the management asked her to leave. She was dismissed from her teaching post for seducing a pupil.
- Stella refuses to believe Stanley's claims, though she admits that Blanche's flighty behaviour had caused concern at home. She blames Blanche's disastrous marriage and her husband's suicide.
- She is appalled to learn that Stanley has ruined Blanche's chances with Mitch by revealing her past.
- Blanche emerges from the bathroom and realises at once that something has happened. She is frightened.

Analysis

Dramatic impact

This is a short scene full of dramatic contrasts. The cheerful mood of pleasant anticipation (Blanche singing in her bath, Stella arranging the birthday table) is shattered when Stanley comes in with details of Blanche's past. His convincing account of her shocking behaviour is constantly contrasted with her sentimental song offstage.

The full dramatic impact of the scene relies not on the details of Blanche's past, shocking as they are, but on her ignorance of what is happening outside the bathroom. Stanley's earlier remark, 'It's not my soul I'm worried about!' (p. 73) has not alerted Blanche to the approaching danger. It seems that Stella's criticism of Stanley's behaviour towards Blanche is justified. Blanche, however, has become accustomed to his hostility and ignores it. Her bathing, on one level a metaphor for her yearning to be rid of her past (see Imagery and symbolism), provides an opportunity in this scene to contrast Stanley's revelations with her ignorance of them. The **dramatic irony** of her carefree singing in the bath, almost within earshot of Stanley's account, plays an important part in raising the tension. That Williams planned this is evident in his use of the musical term *'contrapuntally'* in the stage directions. In music this refers to two independent melodies sounded together.

A01

Progress booster: Driving a wedge

If you are writing about how far a character's behaviour is justified, notice how this scene drives a wedge further between Stanley and Stella. Stanley resents Blanche's continued presence, and his wife's willingness to wait on her. Stella cannot bring herself to believe that what Stanley says about Blanche might be true: 'What – contemptible – lies!' (p. 71). Find other lines showing her reluctance to believe ill of Blanche.

KEY CONTEXT   **A03**

The word 'degenerate', used by Stella to describe Blanche's husband, here means 'homosexual'. Homosexuality was considered a perversion and was illegal, and there was a reluctance even to speak of it openly.

KEY CONNECTION   **A04**

The device of someone eavesdropping on a conversation in which they are spoken about, usually in derogatory terms, is not original; it is employed, for instance, in Shakespeare's *Henry IV, Part II* (1597), Act II Scene Four, where the Prince and Poins listen to Falstaff slandering them to Doll, and make furious comments on what they hear. Williams makes use of a familiar, often-used formula to good effect.

SCENE EIGHT

Summary

- Less than an hour later Blanche, Stella and Stanley are finishing the miserable birthday meal. Mitch's chair is still empty. Blanche makes desperate attempts at conversation, telling a story about a parrot, but Stanley remains sullen.
- Stella criticises Stanley's table manners, and he furiously smashes his plate on the floor. He makes it clear that he resents what he sees as the lack of respect that the two women show him. In particular, he resents what he believes is a criticism of his class from two women who see themselves as better than him.
- Stella lights the cake candles, but this fails to lighten the mood.
- Stanley's cruel birthday present of a bus ticket back to Laurel shatters Blanche. She rushes off to be sick, and Stella reproaches Stanley.
- Suddenly Stella's labour pains start and Stanley takes her to hospital.

 A05 **KEY INTERPRETATION**

Stella's labour pains serve another purpose in the plot. Her departure for hospital leaves Blanche alone in the apartment for the next two scenes, with tragic results.

Analysis

The Kowalskis' relationship

This is a disjointed scene, with changes of mood from embarrassment to violence, to a pathetic attempt at normality, to Stanley's cruelty, and ending with Stella's abrupt departure for the hospital. For Stella and Stanley the focus now shifts away from Blanche's distress.

We see what a strain the Kowalski marriage has been under since Blanche's arrival in their small apartment. Stanley particularly resents the two sisters joining forces to criticise his manners, based on their assumed superiority. When Stella dares to order him to 'Go and wash up and then help me clear the table' (p. 77) he shows his fury by hurling his plate to the floor with the words 'That's how I'll clear the table!' and grabbing her arm. He clearly feels a need to reassert himself in his own home. How justifiable do you feel this is?

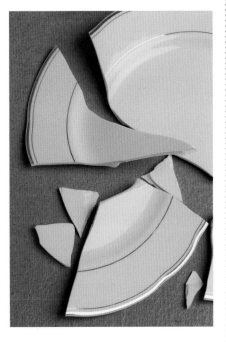

The explanation for Stanley's behaviour towards Blanche, which Stella has been demanding, is now forgotten. (From her words in the final scene, it will never be asked for.) Indirectly Stanley has already answered her when he reminds her of their lovemaking, which is impossible with Blanche sharing their tiny apartment. Justifying himself, he reminds Stella of their passionate climaxes – 'them coloured lights' (p. 81), incidentally shedding light on the nature of their relationship. He brought Stella down from her high social position to his own level, and the humiliation was part of the pleasure for her: 'I pulled you down off them columns and how you loved it.'

A04 **KEY CONNECTION**

In August Strindberg's play *Miss Julie*, thought to have influenced Williams, the footman Jean says 'Fall to my level and then I can pick you up again.'

Dramatic technique

Does Williams use the start of Stella's labour as a device to resolve a difficult situation? There is certainly an abrupt change of mood, with the focus moving away from Blanche. Yet she reclaims our attention in the last moments of the scene. Whether she realises fully her present position or not, she seems different, whispering the repetitive Spanish words in a dazed manner which perhaps **foreshadows** her descent into unreality.

The background blue music from the neighbouring bar plays a much less important part in this scene, and fades out altogether in its latter half, making way for the Varsouviana polka. The polka is heard softly when Blanche is presented with her bus ticket. It is louder and more insistent at the end of the scene when she emerges from the bathroom into the empty room. In this scene the polka is not so much a reminder of Blanche's dead husband as it is a warning of disaster.

Study focus: Mounting tension

A02

In this short scene, with its rapid mood changes, we sense the mounting tension while the characters on the stage (and the audience) wait for the final blow to fall on Blanche when she is presented with the ticket to Laurel. You may notice, incidentally, that it is not possible to experience the same tense expectation while reading the play; the pauses and silences on the stage are inevitably absent as the reader's eye moves down the page.

KEY CONTEXT   A03

Stanley's approving reference to Huey Long shows his working-class allegiance. Huey Long (1853–1931), a corrupt American politician, was nevertheless popular because he reduced unemployment and improved the social services.

Key quotation: Stanley asserts himself

A03

Stanley insists: 'I am the king around here, so don't forget it!' (p. 77)

In modern terms we could see Stanley as the ultimate male chauvinist. He expects to be respected and obeyed in his own home. Blanche's arrival has undermined this, with the two sisters now seeming to 'gang up' on him, criticising his manners in a way that underlines their higher-class background. Do you think he actually feels sensitive about his lack of manners, or is he proud of his behaviour as that of a 'real' man? The play was written at a time when working-class men were taking a relatively new pride in themselves and claiming their rights in the workplace – particularly in the wake of the war in which many had fought, as mentioned by Stanley in the final scene.

Revision task 4: Questions for Stanley

A01

Imagine you are interviewing Stanley about his relationship with Blanche at this point in the play. Make a list of five or six questions you might ask him to pin down what he thinks of her and how his attitude towards her has developed. For example, you might ask:

● Why are you so anxious to investigate Blanche's past?

Write answers to these questions as if you are Stanley – though you do not need to copy his style of speech.

SCENE NINE

Summary

- Blanche is drinking heavily, trying to silence the polka music.
- Mitch arrives and accuses her of lying about her age and her innocence. He tells her what he now knows about her past.
- Blanche tries to explain that her lies are to her the real truth; but realising that Mitch does not understand, she tells him the truth in stark, almost deliberately provocative terms: that, surrounded by dying old women, she used to slip out at night to meet soldiers from the army camp. Then, after the loss of Belle Reve, she entertained numerous lovers at the Hotel Flamingo.
- Mitch says he no longer wants to marry her, but he clearly wants to have sex with her. She frightens him away by shouting 'Fire!'

Analysis

Dramatic impact

This scene marks a decisive stage in Blanche's disintegration. It is effective as **melodrama** as Mitch's hostility and Blanche's half-hearted protestations lead up to the violent ending, with Mitch trying to get what he has 'been missing all summer' – the sex that she has withheld, supposedly because of her old-fashioned morality.

On another level, we witness here, symbolised by the tearing-off of the paper lantern (itself an act of violence), the stripping away of Blanche's pretensions, which reveals the core of honesty in her thought. She knows that she has been lying, but she knows also that her lies are a truthful attempt to present people with the reality they wish for. Though Mitch is incapable of grasping this, she says 'I didn't lie in my heart' (p. 88), 'I tell what *ought* to be truth' (p. 86).

Mitch's incomprehension

Mitch is astonished that a woman as promiscuous as Blanche should object to his advances. This underlines the total lack of understanding between them, which was obvious earlier in this scene when he ignored Blanche's girlish chatter and her pretence of not knowing that 'Southern Comfort' was an alcoholic drink. Both the audience and the reader grasp now the hopelessness of Blanche's efforts to find contentment with him. Once Mitch has shown her, by his clumsy attempt, that he cannot understand, there remains only one way for her: oblivion through drink.

 A05 **KEY INTERPRETATION**

Blanche's identification of desire as the 'opposite' of death (p. 89) fits with the Freudian view that we are driven by the psychic urges of Eros and Thanatos.

Study focus: Reminders of death

Notice how in this scene the Varsouviana music is heard repeatedly. Blanche admits that her awareness of it is an insistent reminder of her husband's suicide, always coming to a stop with the sound of a gunshot. Here the polka stops with Mitch's attempt to have sex with her, and is replaced after his flight with the melancholy sound of the blue piano.

There is also a visual reminder of death in the figure of the Mexican Woman selling flowers for the dead, whose cry of *'Flores para los muertos'* (p. 88) accompanies Blanche's distressing, incoherent description of the deaths at Belle Reve.

Sound effects (the polka music) and visual effects (the Mexican seller of flowers) are continued here. Which do you find more effective when envisaging this scene?

PROGRESS BOOSTER   **A01**

Show that you are aware of the way in which this scene develops dramatically, with Blanche moving from an attempt to pretend that everything is unchanged with Mitch, to her efforts to explain herself, to reckless confession, and then to her resorting to frightening him away by shouting 'Fire!' The drama of the scene is in this development, and it may be less obvious on the page than in the theatre.

Progress booster: Blanche's behaviour

This scene reveals more of Blanche's character. For the first time we are given some insights into her behaviour in Laurel. She admits her lies, but she also tells the truth about herself, even revealing exactly why she was fired from her teaching job – for having an affair with one of her pupils. As the next two scenes unfold, we shall see that when her fantasies meet with incomprehension and brutality, she turns for good to her world of make-believe; as Blanche herself says: 'I don't want realism' (p. 86). What evidence can you find of Blanche's retreat from reality elsewhere in the play?

Key quotation: Blanche begins to lose hope

Blanche tells an uncomprehending Mitch that the hotel she stayed at was not called the Flamingo, but the Tarantula, adding, 'Yes, a big spider! That's where I brought my victims' (p. 87).

This line is open to several interpretations. Blanche has gone from lying about her recent past, to claiming that she somehow presented an idealised version of reality, to describing herself in this surprising **metaphor** as a tarantula preying on men. She is obviously being **ironic**, but why is she suddenly making her behaviour out to be worse than it was? It could be that she is now so convinced she has lost Mitch that she might as well make a bitter joke that portrays her in an even worse light.

Or perhaps she is actually defending her position by ridiculing the way in which she thinks critical men like Kiefaber, Stanley and now Mitch see her. A few lines later she admits an affair with a 17-year-old boy, and to being called 'morally unfit for her position'. Do you think she actually feels guilty, and acknowledges that the pupil was her 'victim', or does she dismiss this? And is her ironic use of the name 'Hotel Tarantula' an angry comment on men misunderstanding and judging her, or just the product of despairing recklessness?

Extract analysis: Scene Nine, pp. 86–7

This scene is the final confrontation between Blanche and Mitch. She, with the premonition of disaster (heralded by the polka music she alone hears), has been drinking, and is dishevelled and confused. Mitch shows his new lack of respect for Blanche by turning up in his work clothes, unshaven, and slightly drunk. In their appearance they both show their distress. This passage begins with Mitch deciding to look at Blanche in the light ('It's dark in here', p. 86). The scene ends with Mitch's bitter admission that he was 'a fool enough to believe' that Blanche was 'straight' – meaning honest.

To begin with, Blanche chatters incessantly and *'laughs breathlessly'*, betraying her nervousness. Mitch's monosyllabic answers are in contrast to her high-flown, artificial speeches. With statements such as 'There is some obscure meaning in this' (p. 86) Blanche resorts once more to the stilted speech of the schoolmistress in an attempt to regain control of the situation. Her flirtatiousness jars and adds to the dramatic tension. Readers (or the audience) expect an explosion of violence, which indeed takes place.

Mitch complains that the room is dark, and Blanche counters with her declaration that 'The dark is comforting to me' (p. 86). The dark hides her fading beauty and, metaphorically, hides the ugliness of the cruel world around her. When Mitch tells her that he has never seen her in daylight, Blanche pretends not to understand him. With shocking violence, he then tears the Chinese paper lantern off the light bulb and turns the light on.

We now realise that Williams intended Blanche's little purchase from the Chinese shop in Scene Three to play a more important role than occasioning her remark to Mitch: 'I can't stand a naked light-bulb, any more than I can a rude remark or a vulgar action' (p. 34). Its real dramatic function is to be used in a metaphor for Mitch's desire to force himself on Blanche. Stripping off the shade is intended to hurt and humiliate her. Exposed to the harsh light Blanche cries out and covers her face while Mitch stares at her. The strong light has shown him her true appearance, and in his eyes exposed also her pretence of virtue and innocence.

Mitch's words 'good and plain' have perhaps a double meaning here: 'plain' can mean 'ugly' as well as 'clear'. Blanche's response 'you don't really mean to be insulting' shows that she is aware of the double meaning.

Light and dark relate symbolically to truth and illusion. The emphasis on light and dark here is striking, particularly as the conventional **symbolism** is reversed. For Blanche light is a cruel enemy while darkness is kind. Mitch believes of course that this is simply because clear daylight will reveal her age. This is true, but on a deeper, more important level for Blanche darkness hides the ugliness of the real world, enabling her to maintain her illusions. When her illusions are lost, so is her sanity.

 KEY INTERPRETATION

In this passage the emphasis is on symbols: darkness and light; a paper lantern hiding ugliness; words with double meaning. This emphasis underlines, of course, the basic theme of Blanche's truth of the imagination.

Blanche is remarkably clear-headed and unusually frank about her preference for illusion. She declares 'I misrepresent things … I don't tell truth, I tell what *ought* to be truth' (p. 86). She is also quite clear-headed about what she does and why. Earlier, in Scene Five, she admits to Stella that she has had to pretend to be seductive: 'put a – paper lantern over the light' (p. 53). The words show that Blanche is aware of her need to camouflage reality. On that earlier occasion she used **metaphors** throughout, evidently because she needed to disguise the truth. Now, knowing that she has lost Mitch, she is recklessly truthful: 'then let me be damned for it!'

Blanche presents herself as an innocent girl to Mitch, because that is what he is looking for in her. More importantly perhaps, that is how she wants to see herself, though she repeatedly fails to maintain this illusion – as in her flirtation with the young man in Scene Five, and in her crude invitation to Mitch in Scene Six, spoken in French.

Mitch's use of the word 'pitch' compares Blanche's explanation to a salesman's patter and shows that her motives are lost on him. To him she is simply deceitful; a liar pretending to be virtuous. The fact that Mitch does not even remotely understand Blanche underlines the complete lack of empathy between them. Their relationship is doomed to fail sooner or later. The way they speak again stresses the gulf between them. Blanche's high-flown, artificial language (especially in the conversation that immediately precedes the passage discussed here) is set against Mitch's short, contemptuous, grammatically flawed replies. Rhetoric against grunts, soft darkness against harsh light – the message is that the relationship would have failed anyway.

The disjointed trivia of this conversation prepares the audience for the reality of Blanche's 'vacation', the mental hospital to which her sister has her committed. Here the **dramatic irony** is revealed only gradually.

KEY INTERPRETATION **A05**

Blanche's words about trying to give people magic, the truth they want, are the only instance in the play of her speaking plainly and truthfully about herself, and it is **ironic** that the man to whom she is speaking is incapable of understanding her.

SCENE TEN

Summary

- Dressed in her cheap finery, Blanche drunkenly tries to pack her belongings, talking wildly to herself.
- Stanley returns from the hospital to await the baby's birth at home. He too has been drinking.
- Blanche claims that a millionaire admirer, Shep Huntleigh, has invited her on a cruise, and that Mitch returned to beg her forgiveness. Stanley mocks these fantasies.
- Fearing Stanley, Blanche breaks a bottle with which to defend herself.
- Stanley disarms her and carries her off to the bedroom to rape her.

Analysis

A nightmarish climax

For Williams this scene was the dramatic climax of the play, with the last scene following as a downbeat conclusion showing its consequences. Here, he uses every means available to him to create an atmosphere of menace (see Language: Visual and sound effects).

There is a nightmare quality to this harrowing scene. The opening stage directions, describing Blanche's *'soiled and crumpled'* evening gown and her *'scuffed silver slippers'* at once introduce a sordid note. As she talks of her imaginary admirers, we become aware that her grasp of reality is slipping. When she breaks her mirror angrily after seeing her worn face in it, we remember the old superstition that breaking a mirror brings bad luck. This warns us that a calamity is approaching.

Stanley's changing mood

Notice how Stanley's mood changes during the scene. When he first returns, half-drunk, there is a moment when he seems to make a friendly gesture towards Blanche: he suggests that they 'bury the hatchet' (p. 92) but her instant refusal restores the animosity between them. It is unclear whether he understands her biblical reference, 'casting my pearls before swine' (p. 93), but he may take it as a personal insult.

As Blanche carries on with her fabrications, Stanley turns on her, cruelly destroying all her pretensions. Her terror takes on a visible form as *'grotesque and menacing'* shapes close in around her (p. 94), mirrored by ugly scenes of violence in the street outside the apartment.

A04 **KEY CONNECTION**

In Elia Kazan's film version the menacing shapes are not shown, nor is the discordant music heard. This omission makes for reality, however appalling.

Sexual undertones

Crazy with terror, Blanche tries to telephone for help, but her incoherent message is cut short by Stanley's reappearance in his gaudy wedding-night pyjamas. His use of the phrase 'interfere with you' (p. 96), with its sexual undertones, focuses on what is to follow. Blanche's terror rouses Stanley to take her by force. The inevitability of it, hinted at by their earlier encounters, is here made plain by his last spoken words in this scene: 'We've had this date with each other from the beginning!' (p. 97). In a way, Stanley is right: the tension between them was always sexual to some extent. Blanche was aware of his coarse masculinity, and we can see her provocative behaviour as her response to it.

KEY CONNECTION **A04**

In the film version (1951), Stella leaves Stanley at the end, taking the baby with her. This punishment of a rapist was demanded by the Hollywood moral code at the time.

Study focus: Is the scene dramatically successful?

It is important to note that Williams took considerable risks by moving away from realism in the stage directions while keeping the dialogue in a realistic key. The question all spectators and readers of this play are bound to ask is whether this scene, so melodramatic in its technique, is in fact successful drama. The use of the blue piano is effective in creating a threatening atmosphere, intensified by the deafening roar of the locomotive. The visual representation of evil (briefly repeated in Scene Eleven) can be impressive in a play that by and large maintains a naturalistic presentation through dialogue and action (though not necessarily through the stage directions); but is it effective when used in one single scene?

PROGRESS BOOSTER **A03**

When considering this scene, be especially aware of the difference between the fixed nature of the text and the broad scope for interpretation. Postmodern critics would tend to take the view that directors should be free to portray Blanche's confusion and terror in their own way, not necessarily following Williams's Expressionist stage directions for lighting and sound effects (pp. 94–5) exactly.

Staging effects

Readers of the play should remember that on the stage the effect of the *'inhuman voices like cries in a jungle'* (p. 95) and sinuous shadows on the walls round Blanche will be less startling to a theatre audience accustomed to sophisticated stage lighting and sound effects, and ready to accept them as part of the staging. Williams's careful stage directions here indicate that he was anxious to achieve a shocking visual and sonic impact in keeping with the shocking spectacle of a man breaking all the taboos and raping his sister-in-law while his wife is giving birth to his child.

Revision task 5: What leads to the rape **A02**

Make notes on how this scene develops from Stanley being apparently friendly, to his carrying Blanche off to rape her. What does this sequence tell you about Stanley's character and Williams's control of the action?

SCENE ELEVEN

Summary

- Some weeks have passed. Blanche is taking another bath while Stella packs for her. The men are playing poker again but only Stanley concentrates on the game.
- Stella has arranged for Blanche to be committed to a mental hospital. Stella tells Eunice that she could not go on living with Stanley and believe Blanche's claims – presumably that he raped her.
- Blanche thinks she is going on a cruise with her old admirer Shep. When the hospital doctor and matron arrive she panics, but is reassured by the doctor's courtesy.
- Blanche leaves quietly with the doctor. Stella stands weeping with her baby in her arms, but Stanley's caresses calm her.

Analysis

Dramatic function

This scene, a downbeat conclusion after the melodrama of the rape, maintains a subdued mood. The arrangement of the play into eleven short scenes enables the audience to accept the transition from the tragic climax of Scene Ten (which would conclude the traditional third Act) to the everyday activities of packing, bathing, card-playing and discussing clothes and accessories. In a sense this scene prepares the audience to leave the theatre.

A03 **KEY CONTEXT**

Stanley refers to his 'luck' at Salerno. This is a port in southern Italy, the scene of fierce fighting in the Second World War. Against the odds, Stanley survived the fighting.

Progress booster: Contrasts and echoes **A04**

Make a note of the similarities to earlier scenes here and how they emphasise how much has changed. Stella has been crying, and the poker-players (except Stanley) have lost their boisterous good humour. More significantly still, they rise courteously when Blanche passes through the room. The paper lantern, which Mitch tore off the light bulb, is torn off again by Stanley and again Blanche cries out as if in physical pain. His action might be seen as a symbolic replay of the rape.

Blanche's daydream of a voyage ends in her picturing her death from eating an unwashed grape, and her burial at sea 'in a clean white sack' (p. 102) – again revealing her obsession with cleanliness. Through most of the scene, we hear the Varsouviana polka, a constant reminder of the early tragedy in Blanche's life. There are visual reminders of the nightmare distortions of Scene Ten, as well as echoes of the jungle-like cries, as Stanley's presence brings back the memory of the rape.

What will happen next?

While recalling earlier, often melodramatic, scenes the mood here remains subdued, up to the moment of dreadful panic when Blanche abandons her daydream and faces an incomprehensible harsh reality. Like Blanche, the audience is kept in the dark about what is going to happen. Only gradually do we come to understand that Blanche is going to be committed to a mental hospital. The doctor's courtesy calms Blanche and restores the subdued tone of the scene. In this calm atmosphere, Blanche goes out on the doctor's arm, a curiously dignified figure. As she says to him, 'I have always depended on the kindness of strangers' (p. 107), her words recall her thanking Mitch at the end of Scene Three: 'I need kindness now' (p. 39); and we now realise the poignant truth that there has been very little kindness in Blanche's life.

Blanche's tragic dignity

Blanche's quiet dignity is in contrast to her display of vanity and her fussing over her appearance earlier in the scene. Classical Greek tragedy demanded for its main theme the downfall of a great person through pride and arrogance (**hubris**). The opposite is the case here: Blanche's vanities and moral weaknesses fall away from her in the moment of departure and she achieves the dignity of a tragic heroine. The effect is to diminish the others in the drama: the sobbing, guilt-stricken Stella, begging for reassurance; the blustering, bullying Stanley; the weak, ineffectual Mitch.

A01

Study focus: Conclusion

Take time to consider your personal response to the end of the play. Do you find the dramatic turn of events effective? The last scene contains elements of **melodrama** – Blanche's ignorance of her fate, her panic at hearing Stanley's voice, her struggle with the matron – but the overall effect is muted. The effect of the trivia of Blanche's wardrobe and her costume jewellery is to heighten the **dramatic tension**. Here again Williams shows the instinct of a dramatist: he creates an ominous quiet to be broken all the more effectively by Blanche's last desperate attempt to escape, and restored again in her dignified departure. Stanley's sensual soothing of Stella provides an **ironic** final comment on events: she has traded her sister for sexual gratification, and the bargain is now completed. Do you feel that Stella was justified?

A02

Key quotation: Blanche's fantasy world

Blanche tells Stella and Eunice, 'I shall die of eating an unwashed grape one day out on the ocean' (p. 102).

Blanche says this just before she is taken away by the doctor and nurse. The words reveal Blanche's fastidious nature: she is worried about cleanliness, and perhaps particularly since the grapes she has been offered are a present from the lower-class Eunice. They also show how, even now, Blanche sometimes assumes that acts of kindness are simply her due as a member of a once-wealthy landowning family. However, the words are also a little flight into whimsy, reflecting a dreamlike fantasy world into which Blanche is drifting in an attempt to escape the harshness of reality.

A02

Revision task 6: Responses to Blanche

Make notes on how Stella, Stanley and Mitch respond to Blanche's situation in this scene.

KEY INTERPRETATION **A05**

Blanche's last words in the play are a direct and most effective appeal for the audience's sympathy and pity.

KEY CONTEXT **A03**

Stella takes Blanche's accusation of rape as evidence of her insanity. Clearly Stanley would not admit it, and at the time it was more likely that he would be believed than Blanche. It was also common at the time for sexual desire in a woman, and especially promiscuity, to be associated with mental instability. Williams had first-hand experience of this: his own sister was committed to a mental hospital and given a lobotomy, partly because of her sexual fantasies.

Extract analysis: Scene Eleven, pp. 101–2

In this powerful passage, from Blanche's anxious 'What's happened here?' to the end of her long speech beginning 'I can smell the sea air', everyone but Blanche knows that she is about to be taken to a mental institution. On the surface it is a scene of normal domestic activity. Stella is packing Blanche's trunk, Eunice is gossiping, Blanche is emerging – as so often before – from the bathroom. The poker players seen through the portières in the kitchen, however, are ominously quiet, in marked contrast to their rowdiness in Scene Three.

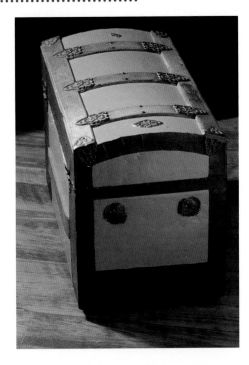

The audience (and readers) are ignorant of the meaning of the scene at first, like Blanche herself. There is complicity binding together Stella and Eunice, and the players, all of whom know what is going to happen.

Blanche's agitated question 'What's happened here?' shows that she senses that something momentous is happening. She is aware of the tension and is frightened. From the words 'Is something wrong with me?' Blanche reveals her awareness that the other two women, who know what is about to befall her, are watching her. The euphemisms 'going on a trip … going on vacation' are cruelly ironic. Blanche's 'Help me, help me get dressed!' is a thinly disguised plea for help as she feels she is caught in a trap. The other two women chatter on, flattering Blanche, complimenting her on her outfit. This is effective as a piece of theatre as the conventional small talk somehow emphasises the underlying tension.

The talk succeeds in distracting Blanche a little. Like a true schoolmistress she offers information about the correct name for the shade of blue of her jacket. The image of the Virgin Mary is of course one of purity, of virginity, and this reference is ironic for Blanche. It reminds us of Stanley's contemptuous response in Scene Five (p. 51) when she says she is a Virgo, and that 'Virgo is the Virgin.' She remains on edge, however, and her unease finds expression in her impatient, rather offhand remarks to Eunice: 'Washed, I said … That doesn't mean they've been washed.'

Blanche admits now that she is aware of the silent presence of the poker players, and fears them. The trauma she suffered at the hands of Mitch, and Stanley even more so, has made her afraid.

When she allows herself to be seated in a chair, Blanche's thought about unwashed grapes starts her on an extraordinary flight of fancy imagining her death at sea, caused by eating an unwashed grape. She sees her own death in brilliantly clear colours, a pretty scene quite unlike the deaths she has described witnessing at Belle Reve.

A05 **KEY INTERPRETATION**

Are the images of virginal purity and cleanliness in this passage successful in underlining the reality of Blanche's position in ironical contrast?

The sketch of the young ship's doctor who will be by her side is strikingly detailed, idealised somewhat in the style of romantic fiction. He offers an ironic contrast to the real doctor from the mental hospital who will presently arrive to take her away. Perhaps this daydream of a pretty death with a handsome doctor beside her has prepared her to accept and trust the real doctor when he comes. The tone of romantic fiction is maintained through to the end of her speech: 'an ocean as blue as … my first lover's eyes'.

We notice the emphasis on the purity of tone of the cathedral bells which are heard in the apartment for the first time now. The pure tone of the bell and the clean white sack in which she imagines herself buried at sea both symbolise Blanche's longing for purification, for a cleansing from her sins, as did her frequent long baths. In the context, however, her dream of purity and of a peaceful death takes on an ironic meaning: the voyage she will undertake on the arm of the hospital doctor will take her to the harsh ugliness of a mental institution, an incarceration that will be a living death for her.

Blanche's imaginary voyage set against the fast approaching reality gives the scene its painful tension. Throughout her speech she is answered by the unspoken thoughts of the others present in a dramatic counterpoint. This scene offers a splendid example of the dramatist's skill.

KEY INTERPRETATION **A05**

There is pathos in Blanche's daydream of a death at sea, pictured in crystal colours as in a romance novel. Again we are aware of the cruel contrast between this daydream and reality. Is it successful as an appeal for sympathy and pity for the heroine of the play?

KEY INTERPRETATION **A05**

The phrase 'silence speaks volumes' sums up this scene: Blanche's nervous chatter and her dreamy description of her death at sea are given their full dramatic weight by the silence of the other players.

PROGRESS CHECK

Section One: Check your understanding

These questions will help you to evaluate your knowledge and skills level in this particular area.

1. How is Blanche's mental instability indicated in at least one way in Scene One?

2. Write a sentence describing how Stanley responds to Blanche in Scene One.

3. What is Stella's attitude to the loss of Belle Reve as revealed in Scene Two?

4. What is Stanley's attitude to the loss of Belle Reve, as revealed in Scene Two?

5. How does Mitch explain the violence at the end of Scene Three?

6. How does the music of Xavier Cugat contribute to Stanley's outburst in Scene Three?

7. How does Blanche express her reaction to the events of the poker party in Scene Four?

8. What is Stella's attitude to Blanche's condemnation of Stanley?

9. How does astrology play a role in Scene Five?

10. What does the incident with the Young Collector reveal about Blanche (Scene Five)?

11. What leads Blanche to tell Mitch about her husband's suicide in Scene Six?

12. What question does Blanche avoid answering in Scene Six?

13. What key information does Stanley reveal in Scene Seven?

14. Explain how and why Stanley helps clear the table in Scene Eight.

15. What reason does Mitch give Blanche in Scene Eight for not wanting to marry her any more?

16. What is the significance of the 'Hotel Tarantula' in Scene Nine?

17. How and why does Stanley comment on Blanche's appearance in Scene Ten?

18. Sum up three or four key events that lead to the rape in the final moments of Scene Ten.

19. How does Blanche snub Eunice in Scene Eleven?

20. How does the Doctor's behaviour help to preserve Blanche's dignity in Scene Eleven?

Section Two: Working towards the exam

Choose one of the following five tasks, which require longer, more developed answers. For each task, read the question carefully, select the key areas you need to address, and plan an essay of six to seven points. Write a first draft, giving yourself an hour to do so. Make sure you include supporting evidence for each point, including quotations.

1. How does Williams reveal the past to be important in the play's plot development?

2. 'Stella and Stanley's relationship is badly damaged by Blanche's visit.' To what extent do you agree with this point of view?

3. 'Despite occasional moments of hope, Blanche is essentially doomed.' How far do you agree?

4. How does the development of the plot lead us to feel more, or less, sympathetic towards Stanley?

5. How does Stella reveal her loyalties towards Blanche and Stanley at various points of the play?

Progress check (Rate your understanding on a level of 1 – low, to 5 – high)	1	2	3	4	5
The basis of the relationships between characters					
The sources of antagonism between characters					
The changes of mood within and between scenes					
Assumptions about morality, class and gender that drive the plot					
The way events are linked and progress towards a resolution					

Tennessee Williams

CHARACTERS

ALLAN _m_ BLANCHE
GREY DUBOIS
deceased

HAROLD
MITCHELL
('MITCH')
*suitor to
Blanche and
friend of Stanley*

STELLA _m_ STANLEY
KOWALSKI KOWALSKI
Blanche's sister

NEW ORLEANS

French Quarter

PABLO
GONZALES
*friend of
Stanley*

STEVE _m_ EUNICE
HUBBEL HUBBEL
The Kowalskis' neighbours

NEGRO
WOMAN

A YOUNG
COLLECTOR

MISSISSIPPI RIVER

A MEXICAN
WOMAN

A STRANGE MAN
(DOCTOR)

A STRANGE WOMAN
(NURSE)

KEY CONTEXT   **A03**

Williams stresses the role of character in a person's actions: the streetcar – or fate – that carries them is of their own making. In traditional tragedy, the hero or heroine's downfall is brought about by fate, a character flaw, or both.

Blanche

Who is Blanche?

- Blanche DuBois is Stella's older sister, who has come to New Orleans supposedly to visit, but it is actually because she has no money, no job and nowhere else to go.
- She is a former high-school English teacher who lost her job because of a relationship with one of her students.
- She is the play's tragic heroine, whose weaknesses, coupled with the failure of others to understand her, lead to her breakdown and committal to an institution.

Blanche's appearance

To begin with, the characters appearing in Scene One are dismissed with only brief descriptions (if any) of their appearance. When Blanche appears, however, Williams describes her in more detail – not only her clothes, but also the impression she gives of moth-like delicacy and vulnerability.

As we read on, her appearance becomes ever clearer and so does her character. Her appearance – slim figure, a face of delicate, fading beauty – is described in the stage directions, and the readers also gather further information about her from the other characters' comments. Indeed she demands flattering comments from her sister, from the reluctant Stanley and from Eunice.

Blanche's faults

Blanche's complex, contradictory character also emerges. Very early in the play we become aware of her snobbery (in her dismissal of the black neighbour's kindness and of Eunice's company) and we shall be reminded of it again in the last scene when she rudely dismisses Eunice's gift of grapes with her obsessional concern about cleanliness – they may not have been washed. She even goes off into a flight of fancy about dying 'of eating an unwashed grape' (Scene Eleven, p. 102).

We also learn that Blanche is a heavy drinker. The reasons for her craving for alcohol are implied, as we learn about her guilt about her husband's suicide and about her promiscuity. Alcohol offers temporary reassurance and dulls emotional pain. Equally, her passion for taking long baths could be taken as a symbol of her yearning to wash away her guilt. Of course, it has a dramatic function as well, her long absences in the bathroom enabling the other characters to speak of matters that are not for her ears.

Contradictions

Stanley gives us the full details of Blanche's past later on, but her seductive manner – which he notes with astonishment in Scene Two and again in Scene Three – is perhaps an early warning. As she so primly insists on her respectability to Mitch in Scene Six, readers will inevitably recall her flirting with Stanley earlier, as well as the episode with the young man in Scene Five. Her actions reveal her character, leaving the readers to draw their own conclusions.

Readers – and theatre audiences – will be struck by the inconsistencies in Blanche's behaviour: her cultural pretensions are designed to impress people with her superiority, and contrast with her genuine love of poetry. She is wilfully ignorant of the causes of the loss of Belle Reve, yet she understands that the root cause was her family's extravagant spending on possibly immoral self-indulgences. These inconsistencies help to make her character less predictable and more fully human.

Progress booster: Thoughts and feelings

A02

Make sure you can write about how Williams constantly gives us clues to characters' inner thoughts and feelings. In her conversation with her sister in Scene Four, Blanche admits indirectly that she knows about sexual desire – 'when the devil is in you' (Scene Four, p. 46) – but it seems that she has never experienced true passion in which love and sexual desire play equal parts. Her incomprehension of real passion is total and will play a part in alienating her sister. The full strength of Stella's love for her husband is shown in the last scene, when she will have her sister committed to a mental hospital, rather than believe the truth about the rape. Passion like this is beyond Blanche's imagining, and it may be that she is too self-absorbed ever to surrender to it. This also explains her inability to understand the effects of her behaviour. After the row with Stanley in Scene Two, Blanche reassures her sister that she 'handled it nicely' (Scene Two, p. 25), yet this is the very point at which Stanley begins to be suspicious about his sister-in-law's past history.

A03 KEY CONTEXT

The young man Blanche flirts with is collecting for the *Evening Star* newspaper. This is an appropriate name. The 'evening star' is Venus, named after the mythical goddess of love.

Blanche's weaknesses

Blanche may hide her alcoholism behind euphemisms but she does recognise some of her weaknesses – 'I've got to be good and keep my hands off children' (Scene Five, p. 57). The weakness that she never does admit, and may not be aware of, is her recklessness, which makes her risk her chance of security – in the episode with the young man in Scene Five and, again, when entertaining Mitch in Scene Six.

Significantly she never speaks of this except when telling herself to be good: her actions on the stage alone speak here. Perhaps this is because she herself is uncertain about her motives for such behaviour. It is not even clear that she regrets her affair with one of her students, beyond the fact that she lost her her teaching job because of it. We can only speculate, and it is arguable that the uncertainty about some aspects of Blanche's character contributes to making her a believable human being.

A03 KEY CONTEXT

Williams himself apparently came to see Blanche as a real woman who went on living outside his play. He remarked that Blanche was a survivor and that he was sure that she would recover and leave the asylum and marry a 'Gentleman Caller' (Tennessee Williams's title of a film script, later his play *The Glass Menagerie*). His own sister never recovered from mental illness. Do you think it is usual for an author to see a character in their work as a real person?

The centre of attention

Though far from being a classical tragic heroine, Blanche still commands our attention. After arriving in Elysian Fields she is hardly ever offstage; even offstage, she is heard singing in the bath. In Scene Seven she happily sings sentimental popular songs in contrapuntal contrast to the damning information about her promiscuity that Stanley is giving to Stella in the kitchen. The same technique is used in the last scene, where Blanche's fussy instructions about her outfit provide an ironic background to her sister's conversation with Eunice about the arrangements for Blanche's committal to a mental hospital.

If you glance through the play, you will find that every scene (except Scene Four) ends with Blanche centre stage, commanding our attention with an arresting phrase or a dramatic gesture. In the last scene particularly, this pathetic, deluded woman assumes the dignity she has been lacking. Her irritating mannerisms, so amply displayed earlier in this scene, seem to fall away, and she leaves on the doctor's arm without a backward glance, speaking her famous line: 'Whoever you are – I have always depended on the kindness of strangers' (Scene Eleven, p. 107). Though the very last words of the play, spoken by Steve, refer to the poker game, they too serve to underline the **pathos** of Blanche's fate, through the unconcern they demonstrate.

KEY INTERPRETATION **A05**

Is the contrapuntal effect of Blanche's singing offstage intended to stress the irony of the situation or to arouse our pity for her?

A02

Study focus: Blanche's status as a tragic heroine

It's important that you can identify how Blanche stands isolated by her ignorance of her future, and by the behaviour of those around her. The pathos of her ignorance has the effect of diminishing those who are deceiving her: the hysterical Stella; the blustering bully Stanley. The change in her status is demonstrated by the players standing up awkwardly as she passes through. This gesture of courtesy contrasts with Stanley's 'Nobody's going to get up' (Scene Three, p. 29), and makes the point very clearly – but on both occasions the focus is on Blanche.

Earlier in the Notes, the conventions of Greek tragedy (see Analysis of Scene Eleven in Part Two), which demand the downfall of a noble hero as result of pride, were contrasted with Williams's elevation of a vain, self-deluded, promiscuous woman to the stature of a heroine. The focus of audience attention throughout, Blanche rises above her degradation and inspires in the audience the pity and fear demanded by classical tragedy. In the end, like the card players, we salute her.

A02

Key quotation: Blanche's fantasy world

'Young man! Young, young, young, young – man! Has anyone ever told you that you look like a young prince out of the Arabian Nights?' (Scene Five, p. 57)

Even while Blanche is waiting for Mitch, whom she hopes to marry, she cannot resist flirting wildly with a young man who is collecting for a newspaper. Her prolonged exclamation expresses her attraction to him and to young men generally, but also her longing for her own youth. It is also typically excessive. Her question is blatantly flattering, but it also shows Blanche's education and her attraction to exotic fantasy. 'The Arabian Nights' is the popular name for a collection of stories originally written in Arabic over a number of centuries.

Further key quotations

- Blanche tells Mitch: 'I can't stand a naked light-bulb, any more than I can a rude remark or a vulgar action' (Scene Three, p. 34).
- When Stanley gets hold of her husband's poems, thinking they are legal papers, she says: 'Now that you've touched them I'll burn them!' (Scene Two, p. 23).
- She speaks frankly to Mitch on their first meeting: 'Thank you for being so kind! I need kindness now' (Scene Three, p. 39).

A02

Revision Task 7: Blanche's weaknesses

Make notes on what you see as Blanche's main weaknesses.

Stanley

Who is Stanley Kowalski?

- Stanley is of Polish descent, though born in the USA and proud of it.
- He is married to Stella, and resents any suggestion that he is her social inferior.
- He could be seen as the **antagonist**, responsible for bringing about Blanche's downfall.

Stanley's impact on others

Unlike Blanche, there is little physical description of Stanley: *'of medium height ... strongly, compactly built'* (Scene One, p. 13). Instead Williams concentrates on his impact on those around him. His intense masculinity and his awareness of his sexual magnetism are at the core of his personality. Other aspects of his personality spring from this pride in his ability to attract and satisfy women.

Stanley is *'the gaudy seed-bearer'* (Scene One, p. 13); confident, and a leader. His garish bowling shirt and his wedding-night pyjamas are the plumage of *'a richly feathered male bird among hens'*. He is at ease with the men around him, confident of his own superiority. He bullies them and they respond with loyalty and affection. His chauvinistic attitude to women may be gathered from the way he addresses the sisters during the poker game: *'You hens cut out that conversation in there!'* (Scene Three, p. 31). He expects Stella and Blanche to sit in silence out of sight while his poker game takes over the apartment.

A02

Progress booster: Stanley's dominance

Make sure you can find examples of Stanley's dominance throughout the play. Stanley sees himself as a natural winner whose right it is to dominate. Even in his first piece of dialogue he is insisting on making a bet on his own terms: *'Naw! We gotta have odds!'* (Scene One, p. 2). Later, during Blanche's birthday supper, he speaks on the phone and insists on bowling where he wants: *'I'm the team captain, ain't I? All right, then, we're not gonna bowl at Riley's'* (Scene Eight, p. 80).

Stanley's machismo and his need to dominate, so blatantly shown during the poker party in Scene Three, are stressed throughout the play, perhaps in order to make the rape more credible. However, we do see a more vulnerable side to him at the end of Scene Three, when he regrets hitting Stella and wants her back. The stage directions tell us that he speaks *'humbly'* to Eunice, but then he shouts for Stella *'with heaven-splitting violence'* (p. 38). Is he genuinely sorry here, or just demanding what he sees as his rights?

Stanley's lack of education and culture

Stanley's ungrammatical speech betrays his lack of education, but he is shrewd, sensing quite early in his acquaintance with Blanche that her behaviour is sometimes quite out of keeping with the character of a Southern lady. He is as acutely class-conscious as Blanche herself. Having married a gentlewoman, he resents the differences in outlook and manner between himself and his wife, although he knows that pulling her down to his level is part of his sexual attraction for her. Conflict is therefore inevitable between him and Blanche, who is trying to

A05 KEY INTERPRETATION

Some critics think that Stanley lacks depth and complexity as a character. Do you think Williams sacrifices subtlety of characterisation to the demands of the plot in his portrait of this sexually arrogant bully? Or does he have his weaker moments?

make Stella revert to the standards of their past life in Belle Reve. It is equally inevitable, given Stanley's awareness of his masculinity and his contempt for women, that he should seek to express his hostility to Blanche through sexual domination.

Our final view of Stanley

The play's construction, with the rape as the climax of the penultimate scene, and the last scene centred on Blanche's tragic fate, influences our perception of Stanley. In spite of his blustering bravado, he is a sadly diminished figure in that last scene. Blanche still fears him, yet she goes out without a backward glance at either him or her sister. We leave Stanley as he tries to re-establish his domination over his wife in the only way he knows, by making love to her.

Our altered perception of Stanley in the last scene may be seen as a testimony to the dramatist's skill. Though his character is unchanged, we see him differently, as do the other characters.

Study focus: Stanley's cruelty   A02

Make sure you can write about the role of Stanley's cruelty in the play. Stanley could, in theory, be dominant without being actively cruel. However, his determination to reveal Blanche's past goes beyond a simple desire to gain leverage to make her leave the apartment. This reaches a peak in Scene Eight, when he presents her with a one-way bus ticket back to Laurel while pretending at first to be giving her an unexpected birthday present. Then in Scene Ten he sneers at her attempts to cling to her fantasy of going away with Shep Huntleigh, and her pathetic claim that Mitch came back to apologise. Then he carries her off to rape her.

Key quotation: Stanley's attitude to luck   A02

In the second poker game, in the final scene, Stanley tells Pablo: 'You know what luck is? Luck is believing you're lucky … To hold front position in this rat-race you've got to believe you are lucky.' (Scene Eleven, p. 98)

This could be seen simply as extreme self-confidence, or as an attitude towards fate. Rationally, no one is lucky or unlucky, but Stanley's belief in his own luck gives him an advantage over others. He is not a career success, yet he apparently sees himself as a front-runner in the 'rat-race' of life.

Further key quotations

- Stanley likes to think he is knowledgeable: 'In the state of Louisiana we have the Napoleonic code according to which what belongs to the wife belongs to the husband and vice versa' (Scene Two, p. 18).
- Stanley justifies telling Mitch about Blanche's past: 'I'd have that on my conscience the rest of my life if I knew all that stuff and let my best friend get caught!' (Scene Seven, p. 74).
- Stanley is patriotic: 'what I am is a one hundred per cent American, born and raised in the greatest country on earth and proud as hell of it, so don't ever call me a Polack' (Scene Eight, p. 79).

Stella

Who is Stella Kowalski?

- Stella is a member of the once-wealthy and upper-class DuBois family of Belle Reve.
- She is married to Stanley, and apparently finds his rough, dominant manner attractive.
- She is also Blanche's younger sister.

How we learn about Stella

We are not given much direct information about Stella's appearance or character. The stage directions describe her as *'a gentle young woman … of a background obviously quite different from her husband's'* (Scene One, p. 2). We learn a little more about her from the characters' comments, especially Blanche's. She remarks on Stella's quiet, reserved manner. Stella's reply that she never had much of a chance to talk with her sister around, though, hints at an independence of mind.

Stella's response to Blanche

A certain dry, sarcastic note may be heard as Stella speaks, but her sister never notices it. For example, she tells Blanche: 'I like to wait on you, Blanche. It makes it seem more like home' (Scene Five, p. 54). Should we take this at face value, or is Stella ironically commenting on how their relationship has always been? It is interesting that in the simple word 'home' she conjures up the world that they once shared. Her reference to it is a reminder that this world still exists for both sisters, even though Stella has committed herself to Stanley.

Blanche treats Stella like a child, a 'blessed baby', ordering her to 'stand up' (Scene One, p. 8), rebuking her for her untidiness, and patronisingly telling her that she is 'as plump as a little partridge' (p. 8). The fact that Stella does not take this opportunity to point out the reason for her plumpness to Blanche – namely, that she is pregnant, perhaps points to her rather secretive nature. She does not spill out her thoughts and emotions in the way that Blanche does.

Stella makes no objection to being patronised by Blanche, other than in her occasional quiet irony, but it is noticeable that she protests instantly at any adverse comment that Blanche makes about Stanley.

A04 **KEY CONNECTION**

Bowing to Hollywood pressure, Kazan's film version ends with Stella leaving Stanley: it was thought that Stanley could not be perceived as getting away completely with rape. It could be argued that this solution greatly undermines Stella's passion for her husband.

A02

Progress booster: Stella's devotion to Stanley

Make sure you can discuss the importance to the play as a whole of Stella's devotion to Stanley, and how the success of the drama depends on it. It is obvious, even without her passionate declaration in Scene Four, that she is deeply in love with her husband, and this love is the cornerstone of her existence. We need to be convinced of her devotion to her husband if we are to accept as believable her complicity in Blanche's committal. To do otherwise, to accept that her sister is sane, would mean accepting also Blanche's accusation of Stanley. If the choice lies between her sister and her husband, there is no question whom she will choose.

Based upon an overpowering physical passion, Stella's surrender to Stanley is almost total: she has chosen to become part of Stanley's life, perhaps gradually remembering less and less of her early life, and accepting her husband's standards, becoming more and more like him.

A02

Study focus: Stella's divided loyalties

Note how despite ultimately siding with Stanley – who is, after all, the father of her child – there are times when Stella defends Blanche. In particular, in Scene Eight, she confronts Stanley for his cruelty in presenting Blanche with the 'birthday remembrance' of a one-way ticket back to Laurel: 'You needn't have been so cruel to someone as alone as she is' (p. 81). She is quite forceful in her defence of Blanche and her condemnation of Stanley: 'Nobody, nobody, was tender and trusting as she was. But people like you abused her, and forced her to change' (p. 81). She even tries to stop Stanley from going bowling, ripping his shirt in so doing.

Stella does care for her family: she is distressed when she hears of the loss of Belle Reve; she weeps when Blanche accuses her of indifference to the fate of her family; and she weeps bitterly when Blanche is taken to the mental hospital. Her *'luxurious'* sobbing (Scene Eleven, p. 89) will not change anything; though as Williams's choice of adjective implies, her sobbing is self-indulgent. She permits herself this expression of emotion, yet she has no intention of trying to prevent Blanche from being taken away.

Key quotation: Stella tries to explain herself **A02**

After the poker party, Stella tries to make Blanche understand her feelings for Stanley: 'there are things that happen between a man and a woman in the dark – that sort of make everything else seem – unimportant' (Scene Four, p. 46).

This shows that Stella wants Blanche to understand what she sees in Stanley, and why she has no intention of leaving him. She does not care that he is lower-class, and she is even prepared to accept his occasional violence – because of her love for him and their shared sexual passion.

Further key quotations

- Stella is vague about Belle Reve: 'Oh, it had to be – sacrificed or something' (Scene Two, p. 17).
- Stella can occasionally assert herself with Stanley: 'Your face and your fingers are disgustingly greasy. Go and wash up and then help me clear the table' (Scene Eight, p. 77).
- Stella tells Eunice why she cannot accept Blanche's claim that Stanley raped her: 'I couldn't believe her story and go on living with Stanley' (Scene Eleven, p. 99).

KEY CONTEXT **A03**

We might reasonably presume that Stella will carry a burden of guilt (as Williams accepted his imagined share of responsibility for his sister's lobotomy and subsequent committal) as a price to be paid for the preservation of her marriage.

Mitch

Who is Mitch?

- Mitch (Harold Mitchell) is Stanley's friend and workmate at the factory. They were in the same regiment in the war.
- At first, he is fascinated by Blanche and wants to marry her.
- He cannot face the truth about her past and abandons her.

Mitch's role in the play

Mitch is the least important of the four chief characters, but he plays a significant part in the development of the plot. Shy, clumsy, slow-thinking, he acts as a foil to the shrewd, loud, domineering Stanley. He is also very different from the poetry-loving, fanciful Blanche with her cultural aspirations. His role is to offer Blanche the promise of a safe haven, to spur Stanley indirectly to find out about Blanche's past in order to protect his old buddy. Also, as Williams hints in Scene Three, Mitch's interest in Blanche encourages Stanley to think of her as sexually desirable; yet another factor in the catastrophic events of Scene Ten.

How Mitch is depicted

We are given no physical description of Mitch in the stage directions. The only details of his appearance – tall, 'a heavy build' (Scene Six, p. 62), perspiring easily – are given by himself, as part of his laborious attempt at conversation. Like his physical appearance, his character is never fully described by the others. The depiction of Mitch's character depends almost entirely on our reactions to his behaviour.

A02

Progress booster: Mitch and Stanley

It is important that you can write about the relationship between the men as well as between the women. Mitch matters to Stanley: Stanley needs his admiration and respect and is unwilling to relinquish his hold on him. This jealousy pays a part in Stanley's determination to expose Blanche and so regain his domination of Mitch. That he is to be seen as Stanley's shadow is shown in his tearing of the paper lantern, and in his half-hearted efforts to have sex with Blanche. Both these actions are repeated by his hero Stanley, who rapes Blanche later the same night.

There is a bond between the two men based on their being in the same regiment in the war, as well as their working at the same factory. Stanley actually refers to Mitch as his 'best friend', though this may be partly in order to justify himself in telling Mitch about Blanche's past.

A05 **KEY INTERPRETATION**

When Stanley hits Stella at the end of the poker game, Mitch does not seem to blame Stanley. Rather, he blames poker. He reassures Blanche that Stanley and Stella adore each other, as if the violence is acceptable. Is he in a sense just a weak version of Stanley?

A well-meaning but ineffectual man

Though perhaps not 'a natural gentleman' (Scene Six, p. 54), as Blanche describes him, Mitch seems gentler, kinder than Stanley's other friends. He is devoted to his ailing mother, and is therefore the butt of Stanley's jokes. He is dull-witted and incapable of understanding Blanche's explanation of her past behaviour. He clings to the facts he has checked out and, hardly surprisingly perhaps, rejects her with contempt: 'You're not clean enough to bring in the house with my mother' (Scene Nine, p. 89).

Mitch's behaviour in the final scene is interesting. He has rejected Blanche, yet he bitterly resents Stanley's role in her downfall. When Stanley talks about believing in his luck, Mitch suddenly bursts out, incoherent in his grief and anger: 'You … you … you … Brag … brag … bull … bull' (Scene Eleven, p. 98). Presumably he means to call Stanley a braggart and a bully, yet he remains sitting at the poker table with him. Later in the scene, we see his continuing sympathy with Blanche when he 'lunges' at Stanley, accusing him: 'You! You done all this, all o' your God damn interfering with things you –' (Scene Eleven, p. 106). Does he irrationally wish that Stanley could have let him remain in blissful ignorance of Blanche's promiscuous past? Whether or not this is the case, he seems finally to be a pathetic figure, sobbing on the table, and too morally weak either to confront Stanley effectively or to save Blanche.

Although Mitch is perhaps not as central to the play as some of the others, his behaviour is important for the depiction not only of his character, but also of those around him.

PROGRESS BOOSTER A01

Although you should write about the characters as they are within the play, and not speculate beyond its limits, imagining how they might develop may help you to analyse them in the play. For example, do you feel at the end of the play that Mitch will simply get over Blanche and regain his old affection and admiration for Stanley, or has his understanding of Stanley changed for good?

A01

Study focus: Could Mitch have married Blanche?

Make sure you can write about the relationship between Mitch and Blanche. Mitch is marginally more compatible with Blanche than the other men in the play. He is sensitive, becoming a little choked with emotion when Blanche questions him about his mother: he can only clear his throat and nod to admit that he will miss her when she dies. He is also a little like Blanche in his continued sentimental attachment to the dead girl whose present of an inscribed silver cigarette case he carries, and his regard for its poetic inscription.

In other respects, however, Mitch and Blanche are miles apart. When they come back to the apartment after a dull evening out in Scene Six, he is unable to make any conversation that might interest her, or to join in her fantasy of being in Paris. Later, in Scene Nine, he is completely unable to understand her explanation of herself saying what 'ought' to be true, rather than actually lying in the ordinary sense. Although early on in the play Mitch is fascinated by Blanche, it is unlikely that a marriage between them could have survived. At the very least, it is clear that Blanche would have found him impossibly dull.

Key quotation: Mitch's moral stance
A02

A disillusioned Mitch tells Blanche: 'You're not clean enough to bring in the house with my mother' (Scene Nine, p. 89).

In this one sentence Mitch expresses both his feelings of love and respect for his mother and his condemnation of Blanche. He says he does not mind her being a little older than he imagined, but he cannot accept her promiscuous past in Laurel. This shows that he shares the traditional male attitude towards women's sexuality. He would like Blanche to be as 'innocent' as she pretends to be – although he accepts that she has been married.

Further key quotations

- Mitch's comment on Stanley's violence is that 'Poker shouldn't be played in a house with women' (Scene Three, p. 36).
- Mitch seems to take a practical approach to romance: 'You need somebody. And I need somebody, too. Could it be – you and me, Blanche?' (Scene Six, p. 67).
- Mitch is bitterly disillusioned: 'I was a fool enough to believe you was straight' (Scene Nine, p. 87).

Minor characters

Who are the minor characters?

- Steve and Eunice Hubbel own the apartment that Stanley and Stella live in.
- Pablo Gonzalez is one of Stanley's poker-playing friends.
- Other characters are the Doctor and Nurse, the Negro Woman, the Mexican Woman and the Young Collector.

The Hubbels

In the opening scene Eunice is sitting and chatting with the Negro Woman. Eunice is friendly and well-meaning, sharing a joke and asking Blanche, 'What's the matter, honey? Are you lost?' (Scene One, p. 3). She is kind to Blanche, letting her in to the Kowalski apartment, and trying to make conversation with her. Even when Blanche offends her by asking to be left alone, she still goes to find Stella. Her kindness is shown again in the final scene when she brings Blanche a present of grapes – and is once again rebuffed.

Eunice is more assertive than Stella. She gives Stella refuge after Stanley's violence at the end of the poker party, and stands up to Stanley on Stella's behalf: 'You can't beat a woman an' then call 'er back!' (Scene Three, p. 38). She also asserts herself in Scene Five, challenging Steve with infidelity, which leads to a violent row between the two.

We learn less about Steve. His main role is to be one of the poker party. However, he does seem more sympathetic to women than Stanley is, telling him, 'Aw, let the girls have their music' (Scene Three, p. 31) when Stanley complains about the radio. He also protests at Blanche being taken to the mental hospital without being told what is happening.

A05 KEY INTERPRETATION

Perhaps the semi-comic characters of Eunice and Steve were introduced to **foreshadow** the Kowalskis in years to come – Stella slovenly, fat and blowsy after too many pregnancies, and Stanley no longer the '*gaudy seed-bearer*' (Scene One, p. 13) but a corpulent, wheezing patron of local prostitutes.

Pablo

Pablo is of Spanish descent, which shows that New Orleans is a cosmopolitan city. He helps take care of Stanley after his drunken violence in Scene Three, recommending coffee. He curses Stanley's luck in Spanish in Scene Eleven, and does not seem to mind his casual racist insults.

The Negro Woman, the Young Collector and the Mexican Woman

The Negro Woman is a neighbour of the Kowalskis, and shows the 'rough' character of the Elysian Fields district: she is seen '*cackling hysterically, swaying drunkenly*' (Scene Five, p. 56) and propositioning the Young Collector just before he calls on Blanche. His role is to demonstrate Blanche's recklessness and weakness for handsome young men. The blind Mexican Woman is hardly a character, more an ominous presence reminding Blanche of death when she cries out selling her flowers for the dead.

A02

Study focus: the Doctor and Nurse

Notice how the Doctor and the Nurse are almost ghostly figures, unnamed and with little distinct personality. Their role is to lead Blanche off to her tragic fate. There is a grim hint of what lies in store for Blanche in the Nurse's comment that 'These fingernails have to be trimmed' (Scene Eleven, p. 106), and in her suggestion that she could use the straitjacket to restrain her. However, the courtesy of the Doctor enables Blanche to depart with tragic dignity.

THEMES

All four major themes of *A Streetcar Named Desire* reflect Williams's own private terrors, and this gives the edge to his writing.

Desire and fate

The streetcar

The theme that dominates the play is contained in its arresting and memorable title. There really was a streetcar (tram) in New Orleans that carried the word 'Desire' as its destination, and another that went to 'Cemeteries'. Blanche's journey, first to Desire and then to Cemeteries, sums up her life, driven by a sexual passion and finally ending up in the 'living death' of the asylum. When Williams was living in New Orleans in 1946, and was working on *A Streetcar Named Desire,* he was so struck by the names of these two streetcars that he mentioned them in an essay he wrote at the time: 'Their indiscourageable progress up and down Royal Street struck me as having some symbolic

bearing of a broad nature on the life in the Vieux Carré – and everywhere else for that matter' (quoted in *The Kindness of Strangers: The Life of Tennessee Williams* by Donald Spoto, p. 129). From the theatrical point of view, of course, such a title was pure gold.

The symbolism of the streetcar

A streetcar running unswervingly along the rails to its destination could be seen as a **symbol** of the inescapability of fate. To Williams, however, the streetcar's destination, 'Desire', carried a more specific meaning. Not just an undefined fatal force, it symbolised a particularly destructive power, that of sexual passion. In Scene Four (p. 46), when the sisters speak of sexual desire, Blanche uses the same image of 'that rattle-trap streetcar'. Stella ripostes 'Haven't you ever ridden on that streetcar?' and 'It brought me here' is Blanche's bitter reply. Talking in **metaphors**, they both know what they are talking about – and so did the author himself. The quotation from the fifth stanza of Hart Crane's poem 'The Broken Tower', which Williams uses as the **epigraph** to *A Streetcar Named Desire*, sums up the misery of promiscuity both for Blanche and for the dramatist himself: 'not for long to hold each desperate choice'.

Promiscuity versus security

Like Blanche, Williams was driven throughout his life from one sexual encounter to another, and again like Blanche he too seemed incapable of committing himself to a permanent relationship. When Blanche longs for Mitch to marry her, she is not seeking a permanent sexual relationship but the material security of a home of her own: 'The poor man's Paradise – is a little peace' (Scene Nine, p. 88).

To be driven by desire, Williams seems to be saying, is self-destructive, yet the victims, whether of one overpowering passion or of the thrill of a string of promiscuous encounters, are carried along helplessly, unable to escape. Blanche's fate is preordained, and the playwright stresses this in the streetcar image. Her encounter with the young man just before Mitch's arrival (Scene Five) and her reckless acting out of a French prostitute's invitation (Scene Six) are a part of her nature, seeming to ensure that she will not become the contented housewife she hopes to be.

The force of desire drives Stella too, who has abandoned herself – and her integrity – to her passion for Stanley. What the final destination of her streetcar ride might be is not shown – except perhaps in Eunice. Stella chooses sexual passion over loyalty to her sister, but staying with Stanley also represents the domestic security that Blanche can never have.

The train as a symbol of fate

Curiously, there is another, similar symbol of fate in this play, one with a very respectable literary lineage. In Scenes Four, Six and Ten Williams introduces a roaring locomotive at a dramatic moment (Blanche's condemnation of Stanley in Scene Four; her description of her husband's suicide in Scene Six; and just before the rape in Scene Ten). The random introduction of the locomotive as a symbol does not carry the impact of the streetcar image.

It may be that Tennessee Williams had originally intended to use the locomotive as the key symbol of his play, but was so struck by the irony of a lurching streetcar in New Orleans with the grand name 'Desire' that he abandoned his original plan.

Progress booster: Interconnecting themes **A01**

You need to be able to write about how themes interconnect. Williams seems to suggest that our desires determine our fate. It is sexual desire that leads Blanche's young husband into his liaison with another man, which in turn leads to his suicide. This is a major factor in leading Blanche into her life of promiscuity. It is questionable what part her own sexual desire played in this, and how far she was trading sexual favours for short-lived attention from men. However, she does seem to desire the Young Collector at the end of Scene Five.

A04 **KEY CONNECTION**

Other writers have used the train as a symbol with considerable effect, usually as a symbol of irresistible power, or fate. See, for example, Leo Tolstoy's *Anna Karenina* (1875–7) and Emile Zola's *La Bête Humaine* (1890).

Key quotation: Blanche's desire **A02**

In Scene Five, Blanche tells the Young Collector, 'You make my mouth water' (p. 57).

In theory Blanche is talking about the 'cherry soda' that the young man mentions, but the sexual innuendo is obvious – probably even to the young man. The image suggests that Blanche imagines in a very sensual way what it would be like to get to know him better.

Further key quotations

● Stella talks about her own passion: 'But there are things that happen between a man and a woman in the dark – that sort of make everything else seem – unimportant' (Scene Four, p. 46).
● Stella asks Blanche, 'Haven't you ever ridden on that streetcar?' (Scene Four, p. 46).
● Stanley contemplates sex with Blanche: 'Come to think of it – maybe you wouldn't be bad to – interfere with' (Scene Ten, p. 96).

Death

The deaths at Belle Reve

Blanche vividly recalls the deaths that she had to witness at Belle Reve, as she nursed elderly relations who died one by one. These memories are with her always: first Stella (Scene One) and then Mitch (Scene Six) are made to listen to them. She gives enough gruesome detail to make the impact of death felt – there is the dying woman so swollen by disease that her body would not fit in a coffin, but had to be 'burned like rubbish' (Scene One, p. 12); and the 'blood-stained pillow-slips' (Scene Nine, p. 88) which Blanche had to change: there were no longer any servants. Blanche dreams of being buried 'at sea sewn up in a clean white sack' (Scene Eleven, p. 102). Her romanticising instinct recoils from the reality of death, but the obsession is always there.

The death of Blanche's husband

The most significant death for Blanche, however, is the suicide of her young husband, for which she feels responsible. Signalled by the music of the Varsouviana polka, which she danced with him on the night of his death, the events of that night play in her mind like a film, always ending with the shot that killed him. The audience hear all this – and the readers have the stage directions – yet in a curious variant of the aside, the other players on the stage hear nothing. Their inability to participate in this tragedy makes Blanche's memories particularly private and contributes to her isolation.

The reminders of death throughout the play culminate in the symbolic figure of the Mexican seller of flowers for the dead (Scene Nine). This figure plays a similar part to the grotesque shadows surrounding Blanche in Scene Ten. The realism of the earlier scenes is abandoned in order to give these symbolic figures the prominence that Williams gave them in his own mind.

Study focus: Stanley's attitude to death

Whereas Blanche is very aware of death, and of her own ageing, Stanley is the embodiment of life and vigour. He only talks about death once, in the final scene. The stage directions tell us that he is *prodigiously elated* when he tells his poker friends that luck is just believing you're lucky. He recalls the high mortality rate at Salerno: 'I figured that 4 out of 5 would not come through but I would … and I did' (Scene Eleven, p. 98). Rather than feeling any sadness about the loss of life, he congratulates himself on surviving. He seems to connect this with his triumph over Blanche.

Revision task 8: Death

Make notes on:

- How death arises as a theme in the play
- How the themes of death and madness are connected

Madness

First signs of Blanche's instability

Blanche's fear of her mental state is first hinted at in Scene One: 'I *can't* be *alone*! Because – as you must have noticed – I'm – *not* very *well*' (p. 10). Never stable even as a girl, she was shattered by the circumstances of her husband's death and by the part she played in it. The harrowing deaths at Belle Reve, with which she evidently had to cope on her own, also took their toll. By this time she had begun her descent into promiscuity and alcoholism. Stella's remark that Blanche's behaviour caused distress at home (Scene Seven) indicates that Blanche's deterioration began earlier, while her parents were still alive. As her promiscuity increased and she drank more, she began to create her fantasy world of adoring, respectful admirers; of romantic songs and fun parties.

Accommodating nightmares

It seems doubtful whether Blanche is ever successful in creating this dream world: the memories of her husband's suicide are never entirely absent from her thoughts. As the sound of the polka grows louder in her mind, the revolver shot puts a temporary end to it. She comes to wait for the sound of the shot to relieve her of the nightmare, if only temporarily. It seems that she has learned to live with this, as she remarks to Mitch in a matter-of-fact way, 'There now, the shot! It always stops after that!' (Scene Nine, p. 85). Her pragmatism in dealing with the nightmares is truly terrifying, as it shows that she has to accommodate the terrors within her daily life.

What pushes Blanche over the edge

Stanley's revelations of Blanche's past (which force her to confront it), Mitch's rejection of her as a liar who is 'not clean enough' (Scene Nine, p. 89), his fumbling attempt to have sex with her, and finally Stanley's violation of her – all these brutal acts break her and her mind gives way. She retreats from the unbearable reality into her make-believe world, making her committal to an institution possible, even inevitable.

Like some of the other major themes of the play – desire, fate, death – mental health was Williams's obsession. He was afraid that he might succumb to mental ill-health because of his sister Rose, whose strange behaviour had long been a source of anxiety to her parents (the anxieties of the family over Blanche at Belle Reve echo this). Rose experienced violent sexual fantasies and made accusations against her father. To avoid scandal, Rose's parents had her committed to a mental hospital and consented to a prefrontal lobotomy (standard practice at the time). Rose's behaviour became more subdued as a result, but she was left with no memories.

A02

Study focus: Blanche's instability

Notice how other characters react to Blanche's instability and eventual mental breakdown in different ways. In Scene One Stella tells her to stop this 'hysterical outburst' (p. 11), aware that Blanche's tirade is at least partly due to her tendency to over-dramatise. However, Stella is aware of her sister's sensitivity and tries to impress this on Stanley. Nonetheless, he reacts cruelly to her growing instability, mocking her fantasies in Scene Ten. The other men show respect for her in the final scene, even when she is led away.

A01 PROGRESS BOOSTER

It is worth thinking about how lighting and sound effects could help convey Blanche's mental instability to an audience. In doing this, you will be forced to focus on her language and movements (as detailed in the play) and it may even be useful in exam answers.

A03 KEY CONTEXT

The effect on Williams of his sister's illness was shattering. Not only did he feel guilty because, being absent from home, he did nothing to prevent the operation, but he also feared that Rose's mental illness might be hereditary and that he too might lose his sanity. He certainly did have some sort of mental breakdown in his early twenties, which contributed to his anxieties later on.

Social class

The DuBois family background

The DuBois family of Belle Reve was one of the old-established 'plantation' families whose members made their fortunes from using slave labour to farm crops like cotton. Many such families foundered after the South's defeat in the Civil War brought about its economic decline.

Blanche's attitude to class

Blanche assumes the superiority inherited with her family name. She is disparaging about the small size of Stella's home, and expects her to have a maid. Most of all, however, she is astonished that her sister has married someone so lacking in refinement or culture as Stanley: 'Well – if you'll forgive me – he's *common*!' (Scene Four, p. 46). She also shows her prejudice in referring to him as a 'Polack'. She makes her feelings about him abundantly clear in Scene Four, after witnessing his violence in the poker party of Scene Three. In her damning account of him, which he overhears, she calls him 'sub-human' and 'ape-like' (Scene Four, p. 47).

Blanche is prepared to overlook Mitch's lack of refinement, because he is at least a little more sensitive than Stanley. However, she does occasionally mock his lack of education by using expressions that she knows he will not understand, such as calling him her 'Rosenkavalier' (Scene Five, p. 58) and inviting him to sleep with her in French.

Stella's attitude to Blanche's criticisms

Stella is unimpressed by Blanche's criticisms of Stanley: she adores him and is having his baby. However, Blanche's attitude is beginning to rub off on her by Scene Eight, when she accuses him of 'making a pig of himself' (p. 77). She has some sympathy for Blanche's fastidiousness, but happily accepts her own life with Stanley. The only time she complains before Blanche influences her is when she tells him not to 'holler' when he throws her a package of meat (Scene One, p. 2).

Stanley's attitude to class

Stanley resents Blanche's sense of superiority. He determinedly refuses to show her any courtesy. He does not, for example, stand up when she enters the room. However, he is at his most resentful when it seems that Stella is being influenced by Blanche, as in Scene Eight, when Stella dares to tell him to clear his place at the table.

A03

Study focus: Blanche's culture

Make sure you can see the different sides to Blanche's character. Blanche is a snob, but in some ways she is genuinely cultured too. She appreciates poetry, recognising the Elizabeth Barrett Browning sonnet quoted in the inscription on Mitch's cigarette case, and seems to be well read: she belittles Stella's apartment by saying it is like something out of an Edgar Allan Poe horror story (Scene One, p. 7).

Elizabeth Barrett Browning

PROGRESS CHECK

Section One: Check your understanding

These questions will help you to evaluate your knowledge and skills level in this particular area.

1. Which characters talk about the 'streetcar of desire', and what does their conversation reveal about them?

2. Why does Mitch's mother want him to marry?

3. Who is the 'gaudy seed-bearer', and how does this description fit the character?

4. Who gives someone a birthday present in the play, what is it, and what does this reveal?

5. Complete the line 'You're not clean enough …'. Who says this, when, and why?

6. What does Stanley say about his wartime experience, and what does this have to do with another issue raised in the play?

7. Who is described as 'sub-human', by whom, and how does this relate to one or more themes of the play?

8. Who mentions the 'Grim Reaper', and how does this relate to another idea in the play?

9. Who anticipates dying of eating an unwashed grape, and how does this relate to other aspects of the play?

10. How and why does Mitch challenge Stanley at the end of the play?

Section Two: Working towards the exam

Choose one of the following three tasks, which require longer, more developed answers.

1. Write an assessment of how far Stanley's behaviour throughout the play is justified.

2. How do you judge Stella's treatment of Blanche by the end of the play?

3. How does Williams explore the theme of death in the play?

A01 **PROGRESS BOOSTER**

For each of the Section Two tasks, read the question carefully, select the key areas you need to address, and plan an essay of six to seven points. Write a first draft, giving yourself an hour to do so. Make sure you include supporting evidence for each point, including quotations.

Progress check (Rate your understanding on a level of 1 – low, to 5 – high)	1	2	3	4	5
The motivations of each character and how these are indicated					
The different interpretations which can be applied to each character					
The way the relationships between characters develop during the play					
The contribution of minor characters to plot, themes and mood					
The main themes of the play and how they are revealed					

GENRE

The unities

In classical drama, there were three so-called **unities**. The unity of time demanded that the action of a play should take place within twenty-four hours. That of place required a single setting throughout the play. The unity of action, less clearly defined, stated that the play should centre on the main characters, with no sub-plots, and that the action should have a satisfying ending. From the fifteenth century onwards the three unities were discussed by critics, and observed – or broken (notably by Shakespeare) – by dramatists. Though not strictly adhered to, these rules still provided a framework within which a playwright could build a play.

Progress booster: *Streetcar* and the unities

It can be useful to be able to discuss how far *A Streetcar Named Desire* observes the unities as a drama. In terms of place, the entire action takes place in the Kowalskis' apartment or just outside it – which helps to give the play a tense, claustrophobic feel. In relation to time, the events stretch over several months, starting in May, and reaching their climax in September, with the tragic aftermath happening some weeks later. They begin at a point when it is not yet obvious that Stella is pregnant, and conclude with the birth of the child. How far does it correspond to the unity of action in your view?

Tragedy

A **tragedy** traditionally focuses on a tragic hero or heroine. This character is an essentially noble person whose downfall, leading to death, is brought about by some combination of a flaw in their character, and fate. The tragic heroine of Williams's play is, of course, Blanche DuBois. The significance of other characters lies in the way their behaviour will affect her. Her sister offers kindness and hospitality, but only as far as her all-absorbing passion for her husband allows. Ultimately, however guilt-struck, she will sacrifice her sister to save her marriage.

Stanley resents Blanche as an intruder in a close, passionate sexual relationship; and she reminds him of his wife's superior background, representing values that he cannot and will not appreciate. Instinctively he sees Blanche as an enemy and sets out to drive her away. Given his character – and Blanche's – the antagonism between them is sexual in nature, and the act of violence through which Stanley destroys Blanche is to him a triumph of his sexuality. To Blanche it is the ultimate breaking-up of her dream world, which will wreck her sanity.

The play, then, presents the downfall of a weak woman who will rise to a tragic dignity in the end. By focusing on Blanche, Williams might be said to achieve a unity of action. Like many other playwrights, Williams disregards the artificiality of the unity of time and instinctively adopts the unities of place and action.

Morality play or melodrama

The morality of desire

When *A Streetcar Named Desire* was first staged (see **Part Five: Historical context**), many critics thought it too full of immoral behaviour. However, the very title of the play implies an element of **morality play**: those who board the 'streetcar' of desire are helpless once they have made their choice to ride in it. In Scene One Blanche changes from the streetcar to Desire, to one going to Cemeteries. Desire and Cemeteries, sin and death – the moral message is clear.

The conversation between the two sisters in Scene Four is explicit about the 'brutal desire' (Scene Four, p. 46) that decides their choice. Blanche goes further in her bitter words, saying that the rickety streetcar of desire brought her to where she is now, destitute and living on her sister's charity. Behind these words there is both self-knowledge and self-condemnation.

Guilt

Ominously the sober, matter-of-fact Stella offers no self-criticism before the last scene, when for a short time she confronts her guilt: 'Oh, God, what have I done to my sister?' (Scene Eleven, p. 105). Moments later, in the middle of her '*luxurious*' sobbing, she yields to Stanley's love-making, compounding her guilt.

Though there is no admission of sin or guilt in the play, we are aware of an inescapable movement towards catastrophe, and that some measure of punishment will be meted out to the guilty. Blanche goes to the mental hospital; we can assume that Stella will continue in her passionate involvement with her husband but her betrayal of her sister will stay with her; Stanley may bluster as before, but even if he can put out of his mind what he has done, his wife and friends will find it hard. The punishment may not be death but it will probably be the bitter taste of guilt.

Melodrama?

A **melodrama** was originally a play with music, but later the term came to be used of naively sensational plays featuring grisly murders, ghosts and villainies. Nowadays we think of a melodrama as a play with plenty of violent action, murders and wicked plots, and characters who are either exaggeratedly virtuous or deeply wicked.

An essential ingredient of a melodrama is its sensational nature. If we consider the leading characters in *A Streetcar Named Desire* – the promiscuous, deluded Blanche; her sister, married to a violent man of a class well below her own; the husband who determines to rid himself of the unwelcome visitor – we find all the ingredients of melodrama.

The play includes numerous melodramatic incidents: Stanley rifling though Blanche's finery (Scene Two); his drunken rage (Scene Three); Blanche's hysteria (Scenes Three and Four); Blanche's revelation of her husband's suicide and its causes (Scene Six); Stanley 'clearing the table' (Scene Eight); Mitch's attempt to have sex with Blanche (Scene Nine); and Stanley raping Blanche (Scene Ten). Evidently there are more than enough incidents in the play to justify calling it a melodrama. And yet if we consider the play as a whole, these incidents are not there to thrill the audience (as in a melodrama). They are introduced to throw a light on the characters and their motives, to explain complex emotions below the surface. Moreover, the subtle and varied language of *Streetcar* is not to be found in a typical melodrama.

 KEY INTERPRETATION

The image of the streetcar as the driving force of passion conveys the helplessness of its riders, but stresses also the element of choice; they have made the decision to board it.

A05 PROGRESS BOOSTER

While the term 'melodrama' is often used pejoratively/negatively when applied to plays, be aware that melodramatic aspects can heighten a work's power. Indeed, many other respected plays – *Macbeth*, *Hamlet* and the *Duchess of Malfi*, for example – also have melodramatic elements such as ghosts, boldly drawn villains, madness and murder.

STRUCTURE

Division of the play

A dramatist must take into account the audience's attention span. As a concession to this, and to the physical stamina of the cast, the convention developed of dividing plays into acts and scenes. In Elizabethan tragedy there were no stage sets, with the author's words providing a verbal picture of the background. Changes of setting were therefore easy. With the arrival of painted scenery and realistic props in the eighteenth and nineteenth centuries, changes of setting became technically quite difficult and also costly. Authors were now expected to limit settings to a few, with each change of scenery dictating the length of an act.

Eleven scenes

Williams divided *A Streetcar Named Desire* into eleven scenes, with no break for an interval indicated. There have been speculations on his reasons for doing this. Perhaps he chose this unconventional structure because he felt that his particular talent was for writing short, one-act plays, and that he could not sustain **dramatic tension** for three acts of conventional length. Certainly if we examine the eleven scenes in *A Streetcar Named Desire* we find that every one of them ends with a punchline or a dramatic gesture. For example, in Scene One Blanche sinks back, her head in her arms, to be sick; and the play closes with Steve's laconic statement, 'This game is a seven-card stud.' The effect in each case is that of the ending of a playlet, with the players motionless in a **tableau vivant**.

Indeed, it is difficult to see how the play could have been divided into three Acts, as only some of the scenes (Two and Three, perhaps Seven and Eight, and Nine and Ten) take place within the same time span.

Structural repetition

The concept of a series of playlets is reinforced by the element of repetition in the play. The deaths at Belle Reve, the death of Blanche's husband, her fear of growing old, her passion for baths: all these are dramatically necessary in more than one scene. Although they are presented from different angles, the repetitions will strengthen the impression that these scenes stand independent of one another.

Study focus: The play's cinematic nature

Make sure you can write about Williams's techniques and influences. For example, the fairly rapid shifts of focus may remind us of another art form – the cinema. We can almost see the camera witnessing one incident and moving on to another, taking in a whole scene or focusing on one face. Apart from presentation, most of Williams's plays share with the cinema their melodramatic elements, the use of sensational scenes of violence and passion. The adaptability of Williams's plays for the screen was certainly not lost on Hollywood: no fewer than fifteen of his plays were made into films, with Williams himself collaborating on the scripts for seven of them.

KEY CONNECTION A04

Williams reveals his preference for the multi-scene format in other works. *The Glass Menagerie* (1944) is divided into seven scenes, and *Camino Real* (1953) into sixteen 'blocks'. Remember that Williams grew up in the twenties and thirties, the golden age of Hollywood. He was also the film critic for his high school magazine, paying close attention to the films he was reviewing, and consciously or unconsciously absorbing their techniques.

The timeframe

How dramatic events are arranged

The action of the play covers a period of some five months. The first six scenes stretch over the first few days of Blanche's visit in May, but Scene Seven moves abruptly to mid September; and Scenes Seven to Ten all take place within one day. The last scene follows a few weeks later.

In other words, there is a cluster of dramatic events in May and another, more dramatic cluster, in September. By this time, some relationships have crystallised: Stanley dislikes Blanche as an intruder and a potential rival with both Stella and Mitch; Mitch is hesitantly courting Blanche. By September, some of the obscure references to the past have become clear too: the loss of Belle Reve; the suicide of Blanche's husband and the reasons for it; the reason for Blanche's departure from Laurel; her hopeless material and emotional situation.

A02

Progress booster: Time

Notice how the first group of scenes sets the stage for the calamities that will take place in the second group; the last scene, which takes place some weeks later, shows the outcome of these events. We have touched on the possible reasons for Williams's choice of eleven short scenes instead of the conventional three to five acts (see Structure). It is also useful to consider here the effect of the grouping of the scenes into two clusters, with the last scene set apart both in mood and in tension. For example, while the first six scenes move more slowly, the violent events of Scenes Seven to Ten follow at a faster rate. The speed of action might be said to play a dramatic part here. You will notice that these scenes observe the unity of time, compressing several violent actions with far-reaching consequences into a single day. Does the unity of time contribute significantly to the dramatic effect?

Scenes One to Six

Though Scenes One to Six set the stage for the second cluster of scenes, their function cannot be said to be purely preparatory. Dramatic incidents, violence and passion figure in all of them in varying degrees. There is perhaps a sense of restraint in the first group (except for Stanley's drunken rage in Scene Three, which can be accepted as part of the usual pattern for his poker nights), of waiting for what the future will bring. The anticipation of disaster is muted, but the audience (or readers) are already aware that there will be no happy ending.

Scenes Seven to Ten

In the second cluster of scenes (Scenes Seven to Ten), Tennessee Williams makes it quite clear that, as Blanche says in Scene Ten, 'Some awful thing will happen' (Scene Ten, p. 96). In Scene Seven we hear Stanley's denunciation of Blanche and her contrapuntal singing offstage, in blissful ignorance of what is being said about her. The tension culminates in Scene Eight with Stanley's cruel birthday present of a bus ticket back to Laurel. In Scene Nine the symbolic – one might say **Expressionist** – figure of the Mexican flower-seller appears, reminding Blanche of all the deaths in her past. It is followed by Mitch's attempt to have sex with her. The audience or readers may be alerted by this abortive attempt to what is going to happen in Scene Ten.

A03 KEY CONTEXT

Scene Three is a pivotal scene of the play. That Williams thought of it in this way is indicated by his choice of the title 'The Poker Party' for the third version of the play.

Scene Ten begins amicably enough, with Stanley even offering to 'bury the hatchet' (p. 92), but soon the tone of the conversation and the atmosphere changes. As Stanley strips off Blanche's pretensions, menacing shapes appear on the walls of the apartment and inhuman voices are heard. The back walls become transparent and scenes of sordid violence are seen in the street outside. The appalling climax of the scene is now inevitable, anticipated by Blanche's terror.

Do the scenes divide into acts?

We could conclude therefore that the differences between the two groups of scenes lie in the degree of hostility and violence that they present. The first group could be seen as Act I (albeit a long one), establishing the characters and the relationships between them, and outlining the possibilities for potential conflict.

The second group might be regarded as an Act II, in which the expected violent events take place. Going against dramatic conventions, the climax of the play takes place at the close of the last scene of this second cluster.

Scene Eleven

Scene Eleven, as a short Act III, presents the aftermath of Scene Ten's climax, but it is just as shocking, as the frantic Blanche struggles to hold on to her shattered dreams and emerges with dignity, at least.

Stella's pregnancy runs almost parallel to the events of the play. We find out about it in Scene Two, and she has given birth by Scene Eleven. This could be seen as providing a different sort of timeframe, acting as a reminder of the period over which events take place, with the birth providing a positive outcome to balance Blanche's downfall and justifying Stella's decision not to believe Blanche's rape account so that she can remain with Stanley.

Study focus: Time as a dramatic device   **A02**

Notice how time is used as a dramatic device in the sequence of eleven scenes. The first six follow one another quite slowly, while the next four shorter scenes move at greater speed, thereby creating the tension of a violent and tragic climax. The last scene maintains the illusion of humdrum everyday activities which is shattered by Blanche's struggle to escape, followed by the restored illusion of calm.

Although at varying speed, the eleven scenes follow one another in chronological order, but some significant features of the plot – in particular, Blanche's promiscuity, her drinking and her part in the loss of Belle Reve – are not given in any logical order, but through indirect references throughout the play (see **Analysis** for **Scene One**).

Revision task 9: How the scenes work together   **A02**

Make notes on how the eleven scenes can be seen to fall into distinct groupings, or sections.

LANGUAGE

Language and style

Two levels of language are used in *A Streetcar Named Desire* – the words spoken by the characters in the play and the text of the stage directions.

Character dialogue

The words spoken by the characters in a play matter greatly, and not only for conveying their thoughts and emotions. The way they speak helps us to form an opinion of their natures, to decide whether we like or dislike them, and helps us to understand their motives. Moreover, the nuances of speech set the characters in their class context and show the differences of social status and education as well as of emotional and intellectual make-up – these aspects, too, will affect their actions in the play.

Blanche, Stella and Stanley

In *A Streetcar Named Desire* the very marked differences between Stanley and Blanche are stressed as much by Stanley's non-standard, slangy, often carelessly slurred speech as by Blanche's high-flown rhetoric which often rings false (as it is meant to, revealing her pretensions) and never lets us forget that she was a teacher of English. At times there is a lyrical quality in her words, emphasising their emotional content. The differences between their styles of speech signal the potential clash between them.

Stella too speaks correct English, but in a matter-of-fact, mostly unemotional tone. However, when she speaks of her love for her husband, she betrays the intensity of her passion.

The Hubbels and Mitch

Eunice and Steve are firmly set a rung or two below Stanley on the class ladder, as much by the way they speak as by their drunken public quarrels. Notice, for example, Eunice's 'Don't she look wonderful?' (Scene Eleven, p. 101).

Mitch too is defined by the way he speaks: his efforts at speaking properly are marred by his genteel circumlocutions – 'I perspire' (Scene Six, p. 62), never 'I sweat' – as much as by his grammatical slip-ups: 'he don't look too clumsy' (Scene Six, p. 62). He cannot follow or match Blanche's flights of fancy – her whimsy about the Pleiades in Scene Six is a prime example.

Study focus: The stage directions

It is important that you can discuss the poetic language of the stage directions – and the fact that it is far more detailed than would be strictly necessary (see Visual and sound effects), ensuring that the sets evoke the right atmosphere. However, they are also remarkable for another reason: they are beautifully written, evocative, accurate and employ imagery to convey their meaning. In this respect they are quite unusual, and provide an extra level of enjoyment for the reader (as opposed to the audience). Take, for example, in the long opening scene description, the reference to *'a tinny piano being played with the infatuated fluency of brown fingers'* (Scene One, p. 1). Make sure that you can write about the language of the stage directions and how they add to the play.

A01 PROGRESS BOOSTER

When writing about characters, show that you are aware of the significance of the specific word choices or turns of phrase used by characters – not just the general sense of what they say. For example, the kind of imagery the characters use is revealing. Blanche uses fanciful imagery, as when she tells Stella that she is 'as plump as a little partridge' (Scene One, p. 8). Stanley, on the other hand, uses more down-to-earth, often insulting, imagery, like his baseball **metaphor** in 'Them darn mechanics at Fritz's don't know their can from third base!' (Scene Four, p. 48).

A05 KEY CONNECTION

The stage directions in Shaw's *Saint Joan* are much longer than those of *Streetcar*, much more detailed and prosaic, yet no more successful in achieving their aim of evoking a clear picture. Why could this be so?

IMAGERY AND SYMBOLISM

The difference between imagery and symbolism

Imagery means **figurative language**, especially **metaphors** and **similes**. **Symbolism**, on the other hand, is the use of something to represent a quality or a concept on the basis of some similarity between the symbol and the thing it represents. For instance, a peacock may represent vanity, or a lion strength. These two examples may be described as conventional symbols, readily understood by everyone.

Imagery in the stage directions

In *A Streetcar Named Desire* the imagery of the stage directions is striking. It is not surprising that Williams makes use of figurative language when he is trying to paint a word picture or evoke the quality of a sound, and to do so in as few words as possible in order to fit the conventional length of stage directions. Thus in Scene One the phrase *'the infatuated fluency of brown fingers'* (p. 1) conveys the black pianist's skilful playing and total absorption in the music. The 'f' alliteration adds to the sense of smooth and masterful harmonising.

In Scene Eleven the Varsouviana polka is *'filtered into weird distortion'* (p. 104) in Blanche's mind. The harsh discords that seem to caricature the dance tune are a signal that the sad memories of the past are about to give way to the harsh reality of her institutionalised future.

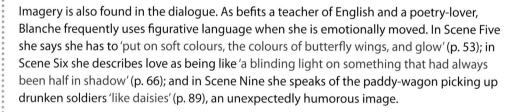

Imagery in dialogue

Imagery is also found in the dialogue. As befits a teacher of English and a poetry-lover, Blanche frequently uses figurative language when she is emotionally moved. In Scene Five she says she has to 'put on soft colours, the colours of butterfly wings, and glow' (p. 53); in Scene Six she describes love as being like 'a blinding light on something that had always been half in shadow' (p. 66); and in Scene Nine she speaks of the paddy-wagon picking up drunken soldiers 'like daisies' (p. 89), an unexpectedly humorous image.

While such figurative language may be expected from Blanche, surprisingly we also find Stanley using metaphors when he is moved. He employs the startling and evocative phrase 'coloured lights' twice in Scene Eight to describe the ecstasy of passion; and when he is brutally destroying Blanche's illusions in Scene Ten, he describes her evening gown and tiara as 'that worn-out Mardi Gras outfit, rented for fifty cents from some rag-picker' (p. 94).

Symbolism

The first symbol to strike the reader is in the title of the play, a streetcar bound for Desire (and then for Cemeteries). The streetcar stands not only for Blanche's headlong descent into disaster, but perhaps also for Williams's lifelong pursuit of sexual partners. (See Desire and Fate in Themes for a discussion of this and other symbols.) The very same symbol of the streetcar is used by both sisters in Scene Four as a euphemism for sexual experience. In Scenes Four, Six and Ten, the headlong rush of a locomotive is another symbol of relentless fate, though perhaps used less consistently and successfully.

Like the streetcar's destination, Desire, the stop called Elysian Fields is an obvious symbol. It is used ironically, however, as the Elysian Fields – the abode of the blessed dead in Greek mythology – turn out to be a rundown street in New Orleans.

Symbols relating to Blanche

The spilt Coke on Blanche's skirt in Scene Five is another symbol, recalling perhaps the blood spilt by her husband's suicide (or perhaps Blanche's 'stained' reputation). Of course, her endless baths stand for her desire to be cleansed of her guilt for her husband's death and of her promiscuous past.

The Chinese paper lantern hiding the naked light bulb is a symbol of Blanche's longing for what she calls 'magic' (Scene Nine, p. 86), the dressing-up of ugly reality. When first Mitch (Scene Nine) and then Stanley (Scene Eleven) tear it off, she cries out as if in pain. The light of the lantern also brings to mind the moth attracted to light, an image used of Blanche's fragility (Scene One).

It is noticeable that most of these symbols concern Blanche, the character with whom many have claimed Williams identified most, and, moreover, one whose great need was to find another, more bearable, reality in her imagination.

A02

Progress booster: Musical symbolism

As well as symbols expressed in visual images or in words, notice how Williams uses music to convey a message throughout the play. The blue piano stands for the callous vitality of the Vieux Carré (also known as the French Quarter) of New Orleans, while the Varsouviana polka recalls the tragedy in Blanche's past. Do you find the use of the polka consistent in the message it conveys, especially in Scene Eleven? The significance of both musical themes goes beyond merely providing a touch of local colour. They mark a change of mood, convey a menace and underline a tragic development.

A04 KEY CONNECTION

Ritual cleansing has a long history, going back to Pontius Pilate who 'took water and washed his hands' after the Jews had demanded the death of Jesus (Matthew 26:24). In Shakespeare's *Macbeth*, the guilt-ridden Macbeth asks: 'Will all great Neptune's ocean wash this blood/Clean from my hand?'

Other symbolism

On another level Stanley and Blanche may be regarded as symbols of the two Americas: the decadent old plantation culture rooted in the slavery system; and the new America of the immigrants – urban, egalitarian, ruthless, vibrantly alive.

Of course, readers of the play have the time to look for other symbols, less obvious ones perhaps: Stella's reading a comic (Scene Four); and the baby's pale blue blanket (Scene Eleven), which tells us that Stanley's luck is in and that he has the son he wanted.

The blue piano in particular can signal a variety of messages, whereas the polka is specifically linked with the suicide of Blanche's husband and is heard by her, and her alone, when she remembers him. The only exception to this occurs in Scene Eleven, when the polka is heard as Blanche emerges from the bathroom, again as the doctor and nurse ring the bell, and finally distorted into inhuman jungle cries that signal the threat of human cruelty. Significantly, they die out as Blanche listens to the doctor's gentle, courteous voice.

KEY CONTEXT (A03)

The painting that Williams refers to in the opening stage directions to Scene Three, by Dutch artist Vincent Van Gogh (1853–90) is *The Night Café*. It is in the art gallery of Yale University, New Haven, Connecticut, where Williams probably saw it.

VISUAL AND SOUND EFFECTS

The visual aspect

The visual aspect of *A Streetcar Named Desire* was clearly very important to Williams, partly perhaps as a result of his interest in the cinema (see Structure). His stage directions are quite detailed, using evocative imagery to convey how the dramatist envisaged the scene. The intention was to create an atmosphere that would heighten the impact of the action – so that you could almost say that the apartment in Elysian Fields is one of the actors in the play.

That the visual aspect of a stage presentation was important to Williams is shown with particular clarity in the stage directions for Scene Three, which specify the vivid colours of the men's shirts, the yellow linoleum, the green lampshade, and refer to a Van Gogh painting of a billiard-parlour. Scene Nine employs the symbolic figure of the Mexican flower-seller as a portent of death.

Sound effects

Sound effects are similarly employed to convey an atmosphere: there is the blue piano with its vague message of the irrepressible, pleasure-loving spirit of the quarter; the Varsouviana polka which calls up and accompanies Blanche's guilty memories of her husband; and perhaps also the roar of the locomotive in Scenes Four, Six and Ten – though its symbolism is less clearly defined and its only dramatic purpose is to enable Stanley to eavesdrop on Blanche in Scene Four.

The only sound effect with a specific function is the Varsouviana polka and the revolver that silences it. What distinguishes them from the other sound effects is that Blanche alone can hear them, an aspect that is very difficult to convey either on that stage or on the printed page. Only Mitch's question 'What music?' (Scene Nine, p. 84) tries to put across the message that the polka plays in Blanche's mind only. Williams tries to deal with the technical problem of presentation here; the truth is that there is no satisfactory method to deal with the problem, unless clumsy authorial explanations are offered.

Could it be argued that Williams deliberately blurs the line between reality and unreality here, for the audience and Blanche?

Study focus: Expressionistic techniques (A02)

Notice how Williams uses the Expressionistic technique of presenting exaggerated and grotesque imagery to express Blanche's mental turmoil. Jungle-like cries accompany the lurid, menacing shadows on the walls in Scenes Ten and Eleven. These inhuman noises represent the confusion and terror in Blanche's mind and, like the polka, are only heard by her, though they also serve to create a dramatic effect on stage.

KEY CONNECTION (A04)

In John Webster's *The Duchess of Malfi* (1612–13) the Duchess's brother Ferdinand imprisons her and tries to break her mentally. In darkness, he presents her with a dead man's hand to kiss in place of his own. He then shows her models of her husband and children to convince her that they are dead.

PROGRESS CHECK

Section One: Check your understanding

These short tasks will help you to evaluate your knowledge and skills level in this particular area.

1. What features make the play a tragedy?
2. To which of the three 'unities' does the play conform, and what is the effect?
3. In what ways is the play melodramatic?
4. What is characteristic about most of the scene endings?
5. How can the play be divided into three groups of scenes?
6. What is unusual about Williams's stage directions?
7. How is the Varsouviana polka used in the play?
8. Who compares soldiers to 'daisies'? What technique is this? What is the effect?
9. What might Blanche's baths symbolise?
10. What Expressionistic dramatic technique is used to express the turmoil of Blanche's mind in Scenes Ten and Eleven?

Section Two: Working towards the exam

Choose one of the following three tasks, which require longer, more developed answers.

1. 'Blanche grows to tragic stature during the course of the play.' How far do you agree?
2. 'A Streetcar Named Desire is really a melodrama.' How accurate is this comment on the play?
3. How does Williams use different sorts of symbolism in the play?

 PROGRESS BOOSTER

For each of the Section Two tasks, read the question carefully, select the key areas you need to address, and plan an essay of six to seven points. Write a first draft, giving yourself an hour to do so. Make sure you include supporting evidence for each point, including quotations.

Progress check (Rate your understanding on a level of 1 – low, to 5 – high)	1	2	3	4	5
The senses in which the play is either a tragedy or a melodrama					
The way in which the events of the play are spread out over time					
The way the dialogue in the play reflects 1940s Louisiana					
The way in which Williams uses symbolism in the play					
The way in which Williams uses imagery in the play					

CONTEXTS

Historical context

Early versions

Williams started work on *A Streetcar Named Desire* in 1945. Early in the year he wrote the first version, entitled 'The Moth' (the metaphor of Blanche as a delicate, doomed moth caught his imagination quite early on). He then put the play aside, returning to it later that year.

He named this second version 'Blanche's Chair in the Moon' from an image in his mind of a young woman sitting in a chair in the moonlight, waiting for a lover who never comes. Blanche took centre stage again. By the summer of 1945 the play had been renamed 'The Poker Night'. As the title implies, it no longer centred on Blanche alone. The comments of the poker players of Scenes Three and Eleven of the final version now provided a counterpoint to Blanche's fantasies. In the final version she is unquestionably the central figure. The card players' gesture of courtesy in the last scene makes it clear that she has achieved tragic status.

How the play changed

The changes in the title indicate a shift of emphasis in the play, but there were other changes as well. To begin with, the family at the centre of the play was Italian, but later the brother-in-law became an Irishman and the two sisters turned into Southern belles. The change is significant, given that since its defeat in the American Civil War, the South's image had been that of a nation mourning for a lost way of life. The two sisters' contrasting choices of lifestyles – Stella's happy marriage to a man from a lower class, who satisfies her sexually, and her sister's miserable promiscuity against the background of disintegrating Southern grandeur – encapsulate the alternatives facing the South and point to the tragic end of the play. The final version is set in 1947, the year when the play was finished, two years after the end of the Second World War.

Publishing history

The play was first published in New York by New Directions in 1947. It was reissued, with an introduction by Williams, by New American Library, New York, in 1951. The Dramatists' Play Service, New York, published an acting edition in 1953. In Britain the play was first published in 1949 by John Lehmann, and reissued in 1956 by Secker & Warburg. It was published as a Penguin Modern Classic in 2009.

Stage history

The play was first performed in the USA in 1947 in Boston under the direction of Elia Kazan, and in December of the same year in New York. Jessica Tandy played Blanche and Marlon Brando took the part of Stanley. Later Blanche was played in turn by Uta Hagen and Tallulah Bankhead (herself a Southerner from Alabama) while Brando was replaced for a time by Anthony Quinn. The British premiere was in 1949 at the Aldwych Theatre in London under the direction of Laurence Olivier.

KEY CONTEXT **A03**

In the final version the brother-in-law becomes a Polish-American. Many of the Polish immigrants before the 1940s and 1950s were not political refugees, or middle class – they were labourers, mostly uneducated, who were looked down upon. The change was made to emphasise the class element in the play, which adds another dimension to the sexual tension between Blanche and Stanley.

KEY CONNECTION **A04**

If you are unable to see the play on stage, watch the 1951 film version of the play, directed by Elia Kazan. Vivien Leigh and Marlon Brando played the leading parts to considerable acclaim. Alternatively the 1995 TV film version (dir. Glenn Jordan) is more faithful to the script – and therefore a half-hour longer.

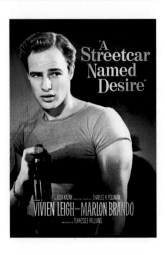

The Second World War (1939–45)

Although Williams was working on *A Streetcar Named Desire* at the end of the Second World War, and the play was first staged in 1947, only two years after the war, there is hardly any mention of the recent cataclysmic events in it – only Stanley's brief reference to the Salerno landings in Scene Eleven. Indeed, the political changes that followed the Second World War, which included the Cold War and the rise of the United States as a world power, are notable for their omission. This omission is characteristic of all Williams's plays and seems to emphasise that the plays exist in their own world and time. The resulting claustrophobic quality contributes to the dramatic tension they all share.

American Civil War (1861–5)

The events that did indirectly affect Williams, like most Southerners, were those of the American Civil War. In spite of the romantic aura that surrounded it, the primary concerns of the Civil War were economic. First and foremost, there was the issue of slavery. Slavery was seen as an evil in the North, but the Southern states regarded it as essential for the tobacco and cotton industries on which their wealth was founded. When Abraham Lincoln was elected president in 1860, wanting to keep the union from breaking up, he promised the Southern states that slavery would continue to be legal in the states where it already existed. At first the Northern half of the United States wanted only to stop slavery spreading to other states but gradually, as the anti-slavery feeling grew stronger, total abolition of slavery became the declared aim of the North.

Another economic question that divided the South from the North was the demand of the American manufacturing industry, based largely in the North, for a tax on imported goods. The Southern states regarded this as an infringement of their rights and threatened to secede from the union.

There had been unrest among the slaves, and the slave-owning states felt themselves to be increasingly under threat. The break-up of the union became a reality as, one by one, seven Southern states (Georgia, Alabama, Florida, Mississippi, Louisiana, South Carolina and Texas) seceded, forming the Confederate States of America. After a Southern attack on Fort Sumter in South Carolina, which was held by Union (Northern) troops, President Lincoln denounced the Confederate states as rebels. Four more Southern states broke away (Virginia, North Carolina, Arkansas and Tennessee), and the war began.

A03 KEY CONTEXT

The author Mark Twain, himself for many years a Mississippi pilot, once said that in the South the Civil War 'is what AD is elsewhere, they date from it'.

A03 KEY CONTEXT

The Northerners moving in were nicknamed 'carpetbaggers' because they would arrive with only a carpetbag of personal belongings to further their political careers and make their fortunes.

The war ended with Confederate surrender in April 1865. By then, much of the South lay in ruins and though Lincoln hoped to 'bind up the South's wounds', he was assassinated a few days after the surrender, shot by an actor, John Wilkes Booth – a man with a deep hatred of the Union.

As a result, the treatment of the South was very harsh, and it took a long time for it to recover, especially when slavery was finally abolished a few years later. There is no doubt that the Southern defeat was exploited by Northerners moving in, which added to the bitterness of defeat. In economic decline, the South soon came to exercise an enduring influence on the imagination of writers in the South, and in the North as well.

KEY CONNECTION   A04

Rose Macaulay's 1932 novel *They Were Defeated* is about the Royalist defeat in the English Civil War – comparable to the defeat of the Confederate states by the North. Sir Walter Scott's *Waverley* (1814) and *Redgauntlet* (1824), and R. L. Stevenson's *Kidnapped* (1886) and *Catriona* (1893) all have a Jacobite background.

Homosexuality and the law

Uninterested in writing about the Second World War, Williams seemed equally indifferent to the inclusion of a political issue that had gained greatly in significance during his lifetime, and which might have been expected to have touched him closely: the question of gay rights. The politicising of what was seen as a moral issue was successful in achieving its aims, and its impact on literature and the performing arts was great. Yet Williams appeared unmoved by the movement or by its success.

The issue of homosexuality, so prominent in his private life (see below), is clearly a strand in his work, but never the central theme, and certainly never taken up to be defended or pleaded for. We must remember, of course, that for the greater part of Williams's life homosexuality was still illegal, though tolerated in some areas (New Orleans; Key West, Florida). This might explain his reluctance to give prominence to the issue.

Williams's attitude to homosexuality

According to Christopher Isherwood and others, there might have been another reason for Williams's refusal to take up the cause of homosexuality. They maintain that he hated being a homosexual, and could not accept those who came to terms with their sexual orientation (see *The Kindness of Strangers: The Life of Tennessee Williams* by Donald Spoto, p. 320).

When accused of never dealing with homosexuality openly, Williams declared in an interview with *Gay Sunshine* that the main focus of his work was not sexual orientation but social issues: 'I am not about to limit myself to writing about gay people' (quoted in *The Kindness of Strangers: The Life of Tennessee Williams* by Donald Spoto, p. 319). The statement is open to doubt; homosexuality plays an important part in his plays, even when not openly discussed, and he deals with social issues only in their most general sense of class snobbery; the resentment felt by people who see themselves as despised for their lack of social skills.

Even if he disapproved, he felt compelled to introduce homosexuality into his plays. Blanche, for example, might equally have found her husband in bed with a woman, though of course the dramatic effect would have been less shocking. In several of his plays we sense a condemnation of homosexuality (*A Streetcar Named Desire*, *Cat on a Hot Tin Roof*, *Suddenly Last Summer*).

A conflict existed, then, between his morality and his sexuality – never to be resolved, and never to be brought into the open in his plays, though the subject of gay rights was very much in the foreground politically in the United States, especially during Williams's later years.

Revision task 10: Contextual influences

List the main contextual influences on *A Streetcar Named Desire* and how they are reflected in the play.

Setting

New Orleans

The whole play is set in an apartment in the French Quarter (also known as the Vieux Carré) of the city of New Orleans, in the state of Lousiana. New Orleans features most vividly in the opening stage directions. Williams describes the district with considerable affection. It lies between the Mississippi River and the L&N railway tracks – drily mentioned by Stella in Scene One, and which probably explains why it is a poor area. However, Williams adds that, *'unlike corresponding sections in other American cities, it has a raffish charm'* (Scene One, p. 1). In other words its charm lies in its being carefree, fun-loving and unconventional. This idea is reinforced by Williams's description of the *'music of Negro entertainers'*, which characterises the area, and which *'expresses the spirit of the life which goes on here'*. However, Williams also mentions *'the atmosphere of decay'*, suggesting that this area, like the South in general, has seen better days. The building in which the Kowalskis live was probably at one time occupied by one family, but now, as in buildings in so many inner city areas, it is divided up into two flats. The Kowalskis live in the downstairs one.

Elysian Fields

The fact that the Kowalskis live in the French Quarter creates a relaxed atmosphere at the start of the play. Their street being called Elysian Fields also fits in with the atmosphere. In Greek myth the Elysian Fields were the area of the Underworld reserved for dead heroes – a sort of retirement playground for the virtuous. Hence we see Stanley going bowling, playing poker and drinking, but we never see him at work. In fact he barely even mentions work.

Ethnic diversity

One obvious result of the play being set in a city – and particularly in this district, is its ethnic diversity and tolerance. The play begins with the white Eunice and an unnamed black woman chatting outside the house. That this was relatively unusual in America at the time is shown by Williams explaining: *'New Orleans is a cosmopolitan city where there is a relatively warm and easy intermingling of races in the old part of town.'* The diversity is also seen in Stanley, with his Polish background; Pablo, whose first language is Spanish; and in the Mexican street vendors.

The apartment

It is a strong feature of the play that it is set entirely in the Kowalski apartment – or occasionally just outside it. It is small, consisting of a room which is *'primarily a kitchen but contains a folding bed to be used by Blanche'* (Scene One, p. 4), a bedroom and the bathroom in which Blanche spends so much of her time. There is little privacy for either Blanche or the Kowalskis in the apartment, which is a problem for Blanche, but even more so for Stanley and Stella because it inhibits their sex life.

A03 KEY CONTEXT

Blanche has been living in a hotel in Laurel. Williams may have had in mind the real town of Laurel, about 200 miles west of New Orleans. It is small enough for Blanche's reputation to become widely known in the town.

Literary context

The effects of the Civil War

After the defeat of the Confederate army in 1865, the literature of the South revived gradually and began to thrive on the nostalgia for the past, on regional rather than national patriotism and on the romantic appeal of a lost cause and a lost way of life. A comparison might be made here with the romantic appeal of the defeated Royalists, the Cavaliers of seventeenth-century England, and of the Jacobite cause in Scotland.

The romanticising of the South continued into the twentieth century, a tendency boosted by Margaret Mitchell's famous 1936 novel *Gone with the Wind*, and especially as a result of the phenomenal success of the 1939 film version of the novel.

Independent of this popular romantic image of the South, a new, separate, specifically Southern literature, The 'Mississippi School', emerged in the twentieth century. The fascination with the past merged gradually with an awareness of a South whose economic decay was symbolised by the fading beauty of the planters' mansions (like Williams's Belle Reve).

Greed and treachery were described as part of the Southern character in the novels of William Faulkner, set in the imaginary Yoknapatawpha County, and those of Thomas Wolfe, Erskine Caldwell and Williams's friend Carson McCullers.

Southern Gothic

One quality regarded as characteristic of the Southern writers was their rich imagination, often bordering on the bizarre and the grotesque – 'Southern Gothic' was the phrase used to describe it. Its inspiration lay perhaps in an awareness of belonging to a dying culture – dashing, romantic, but at the same time living in an economy based on deep injustice and cruelty. The contradiction inherent in the cultural climate favoured the individualistic, the eccentric and the outcast.

This was the Southern culture that appealed to Tennessee Williams. His dislike of his mother had an adverse effect on his attitude to the romanticised South, but the South as a broken, damaged society with the ripe charms of decay fired his imagination. As he himself said, 'I write out of love for the South … once a way of life that I am just old enough to remember – not a society based on money … I write about the South because I think the war between romanticism and the hostility to it is very sharp there' (quoted in *The Kindness of Strangers: The Life of Tennessee Williams* by Donald Spoto, p. 139). The South seemed to him to stand for cultural values ignored by the money-grabbing, prosperous North of the carpetbaggers – thus Blanche and Stanley may be seen as representing the two opposing sides.

European influences

The subject matter of Williams's plays was deeply influenced by his image of the South, but he looked to the playwrights of Europe for models of the form. When a student at the University of Missouri, and already dreaming of a career as a playwright, Tennessee Williams immersed himself in the plays of Anton Chekhov, August Strindberg and Henrik Ibsen. August Strindberg's *Miss Julie* (1888) may well have influenced *A Streetcar Named Desire* in its equation of class antagonism with sexual tension.

Again, a parallel may be drawn between the plantation culture of Belle Reve and the household of Madame Ranevskaya in Anton Chekhov's *The Cherry Orchard* (1904). Both are doomed, useless, their extravagant existence based on the labour of others, yet they both possess a charm and romantic appeal lacking equally in the blustering merchant Lopakhin in *The Cherry Orchard* and in Stanley Kowalski.

As for Henrik Ibsen, Tennessee Williams could have wished for no better models for constructing a play around one compelling central character than *A Doll's House* (1879), *Hedda Gabler* (1890), *The Master Builder* (1892) or *John Gabriel Borkman* (1896), to name a few among many.

The two cultures – the Southern and the European – meet successfully in *A Streetcar Named Desire*, in its Southern setting and its romantic doomed heroine Blanche DuBois, with her class pretensions and European-sounding name.

Modern connections

There are some other modern texts that share the themes of madness and power with *A Streetcar Named Desire*. In the world of theatre, Arthur Miller's *The Crucible* (1953) is set in an early New England community and is based on witch trials that actually took place. The mental disturbance in Miller's play lies in a group of teenage girls who imagine, or are persuaded to claim, that they have seen various local people consorting with the Devil. The play also features issues of loyalty and betrayal, as does Miller's play *A View from the Bridge* (1955). This could be compared with the decision Stella has to make as to whether to stay with Stanley or side with Blanche. Miller's plays, however, are more politically motivated than *A Streetcar Named Desire*.

A prose text in which these same themes emerge is Ken Kesey's *One Flew Over the Cuckoo's Nest* (1975). In this novel, set in a men's mental hospital, the working-class **protagonist**, McMurphy, is locked into a battle of wills with the controlling and manipulative Nurse Ratched. In some ways this battle could be compared with the conflict between Stanley and Blanche. The rebellious McMurphy disrupts the controlled calm of the mental hospital; Blanche disrupts the status quo in the Kowalskis' household. McMurphy is eventually given brain-deadening electric shock treatment; Blanche suffers a breakdown, partly at least because of being raped.

Another novel with links to *A Streetcar Named Desire* is Maggie O'Farrell's *The Vanishing Act of Esme Lennox* (2006). In this, a teenage girl who refuses to conform has an apparent mental breakdown as a result of being raped by her sister's suitor. She then spends most of her life in a mental hospital, which seems to be convenient for her family.

Connections relating to social class could be found in Arundhati Roy's *The God of Small Things*, set in a class-bound India, and particularly concerned with how what is left of the caste system there still binds relationships.

A05 KEY CONNECTION

Unlike the relationship between Stanley and Blanche, that between Madame Ranevskaya and Lopakhin in Chekhov's *The Cherry Orchard* contains no sexual undertones. Chekhov focuses on social issues: Lopakhin is a peasant who acquires wealth, Madame Ranevskaya a noble from a family in decline.

A04 KEY CONNECTION

Williams wrote another play set in the French Quarter of New Orleans: the autobiographical *Vieux Carré*. It was first performed in 1977, on Broadway. It closed after only five performances.

CRITICAL INTERPRETATIONS

Early reception

Cinema and the South

A Streetcar Named Desire was written and staged in the 1940s, when American cinema was at the height of its popularity, and theatre audiences were deeply influenced – one might say conditioned – by the movies. The play was a mixture of sex, violence and (implicit) morality; a recipe tested out successfully in the cinema. The play drew also on the romantic myth of the American South, as did Williams's first successful play, *The Glass Menagerie*. This myth was reinforced by the fantastic success of MGM's *Gone with the Wind* (1939), starring Vivien Leigh. Though Williams did not accept the romanticised view of the South uncritically, he undoubtedly made use of it in the tragic figure of Blanche DuBois.

KEY CONNECTION   A04

Williams makes reference to his staging innovations in his preface to *The Glass Menagerie*, where he explains his 'unconventional techniques' of using screen images and titles in the play, and his 'conception of a new, plastic theatre' so that the theatre would 'resume vitality as part of our culture'.

The Glass Menagerie

The much-praised staging of *The Glass Menagerie* (premiered in Chicago in 1944, and transferred in 1945 to New York where it ran for 561 performances) raised the expectations of both the theatre critics and the audiences for Williams's follow-up play. There was a readiness in the audience to accept a play that departed considerably from the accepted formula of the traditional 'well-made play' and used unexpected, non-realistic methods to stress what the playwright regarded as the play's significant scenes and values.

In *The Glass Menagerie* Williams uses the projection of screen images and titles, and introduces a recurrent tune, 'The Glass Menagerie'. Though he abandoned the use of screen images in the acting version of the play, his intention to use them is significant, and makes understandable his use of Expressionist evil shapes and jungle-like cries, as well as of the blue piano and Varsouviana polka in *A Streetcar Named Desire*.

KEY CONTEXT   A03

Eugene O'Neill (1888–1956), to whom Williams was compared, was an internationally renowned American dramatist, who enjoyed success in the Thirties. His most famous play is probably *The Iceman Cometh* (published 1939, staged 1946).

Positive reviews of *A Streetcar Named Desire*

After previews in Boston, New Haven and Philadelphia, *A Streetcar Named Desire* opened in New York on 3 December 1947. The reception was very favourable. Richard Watts Jr., in the *New York Post* of 4 December 1947, hailed its author as 'an oncoming playwright of power, imagination and an almost desperately morbid turn of mind and emotion', while Louis Kromberger in *PM* of 5 December 1947 described *A Streetcar Named Desire* as 'an enormous advance over that minor-key and too wet-eyed work, *The Glass Menagerie*'.

There was a glowing review by the doyen of New York critics, Brooks Atkinson, in the *New York Times* on 4 December 1947, in which he also pointed out that Williams presented the theatre with considerable problems because of his avoidance of conventional form. Indeed, some reviewers criticised the episodic nature of the play, failing to recognise its significance for the theatre of the future. In the *New York Herald Tribune* of 4 December 1947 Howard Barnes praised Williams as 'the Eugene O'Neill of the present period'. Harold Clurman in *Tomorrow*, February 1948, stressed the impact of *A Streetcar Named Desire* as 'especially strong because it is virtually unique as a stage piece that is both personal and social'.

Less positive reviews

There were also some less complimentary reviews, notably by Ward Morehouse in the *Sun* (a New York newspaper), 4 December 1947, in which *A Streetcar Named Desire* was described as 'not a play for the squeamish', recalling the phrase 'an almost desperately morbid turn of mind' in the otherwise favourable review by Richard Watts Jr. mentioned above.

Time (15 December 1947) declared that 'the play could stand more discipline … There is sometimes an absence of form. And it could stand more variety; only the clash between Blanche and Stanley gets real emotion and drama into the play.' *Time* went on giving negative notices to Williams's plays until 1962, when it suddenly called him 'the greatest living playwright anywhere'.

A05

Study focus: How *A Streetcar Named Desire* broke new ground

It is important you can write about how ground-breaking the play was when it was written. What was new in *A Streetcar Named Desire* was the combination of realism and lyricism. To some extent this was the obvious result of presenting in the same play a character like Blanche who lives in a dream world and uses the language of a schoolteacher and a poetry-lover, and characters like Stanley and Steve, uneducated men whose world is circumscribed by drinking, card-playing and chasing women. Yet this is not simply a matter of pitting an educated speaker against an uneducated one.

The psychology of the characters is realistic, and their motives and action seem wholly credible, taken scene by scene, but as the action moves inexorably to the climax of Scene Ten it rises above everyday reality into the realm of high tragedy. Mirroring the change in the characters and the action, the setting too, entirely realistic at first – a two-room apartment with a bathroom in a shabby house in New Orleans – undergoes a change. The walls dissolve, lurid shapes appear and jungle noises are heard.

As the characters and the setting change, they appear less predictable and their unexpected ambiguity heightens the dramatic tension. The dramatic potential of unpredictability, and the essential mystery of human nature are exploited here, as they will be in a much more sensational form in Williams's later plays. Yet the sensationalism that was often seized upon by the critics is in the end not what characterises Williams's work. It can be argued that what the audience senses is the terrifying mystery, the changeability of human nature, the unpredictability of fate. Make sure you can write about the mixture of realism and lyricism in the play.

Reception in Britain

In England *A Streetcar Named Desire* was mostly well received after its British premiere on 12 October 1949, under the direction of Laurence Olivier, with Vivien Leigh as Blanche, Bonar Colleano as Stanley, Renée Asherson as Stella and Bernard Braden as Mitch. There were glowing reviews in the *Daily Express* and the *Evening Standard* and in the quality weeklies (for instance R. D. Smith's review in the *New Statesman & Nation* on 22 October 1949). Harold Hobson in the *Sunday Times* of 13 November 1949 described it as 'strictly and even puritanically' a valuable play.

The reviews seemed to focus on the sexual aspect of the play. Thus J. C. Trewin in the *Illustrated London News* dismissed *A Streetcar Named Desire* as 'a squalid anecdote of a nymphomaniac's decay in a New Orleans slum'. Such condemnations are particularly noteworthy when we remember that they came after the cuts in the text made as a result of censorship.

A03 **KEY CONTEXT**

The realism of the setting (a shabby apartment in a rundown house) and of the characters (factory workers and a schoolteacher out of a job) contrasts with the unexpected feasts of lyricism in the dialogue and the high drama of the last three scenes.

A03 **KEY CONTEXT**

Jean Cocteau's adaptation of *A Streetcar Named Desire* opened in Paris as *Un Tramway Nommé Désir*. Perhaps surprisingly, in view of the popular idea of French tolerance, many disapproving voices were heard. Thus André Alter in *L'Aube* of 20 October 1949 spoke of the frightening emptiness and the shallowness of the play, which even Lila de Nobili's designs failed to fill. Jean-Jacques Gautier in the *Figaro* of 19 October 1949 described the play as 'filled with undressing, morbid events, fights and games … obscenities and murders'.

Later revivals

An American classic

Though seen by many as sensationalist to begin with, over the years *A Streetcar Named Desire* came to be regarded as an American classic, almost a part of American popular culture. Stanley's drunken bellow of 'STELLL-LAHHHHH' (Scene Three, p. 38) and Blanche's poignant last words in the play 'I have always depended on the kindness of strangers' (Scene Eleven, p. 107) were remembered and quoted.

US productions

Perhaps not surprisingly, in the United States the play has been revived many times since its first staging in New York in 1947, for the last time (at the time of going to press) in 2009. The revivals attracted attention, though not always praise. The most notable among them was the 1949–50 Road Company production with Uta Hagen and Anthony Quinn. In 1956 came the New York staging with Tallulah Bankhead and Gerald O'Loughlin. There were also innovative multi-racial and all-black productions in 1953, 1956 and 1958.

In 1973 a revival in Los Angeles was directed by James Bridges, with Faye Dunaway as Blanche and Jon Voight as Stanley. Stephen Faber in the *New York Times* of 1 April 1973 cruelly dismissed Voight's performance: 'Voight's studious attempt to underplay the role is disastrous. His relatively quiet, halting ineffectual Stanley makes little sense on any level. He even throws dishes politely. Voight simply has no menace; he never believes he has the power to destroy Blanche.'

Another New York revival came in 1973 at the Lincoln Center, with Rosemary Harris and James Farentino in the leading roles. In 1988 another production was staged in New York under the direction of Nikos Psacharopoulos, with Blythe Danner as Blanche and Aidan Quinn as Stanley. Edith Oliver's review in the *New Yorker*, March 1988, was interesting, though not particularly complimentary: Quinn's Stanley was seen by her as 'too much a man of the eighties to make sex seem menacing'.

There was a major revival in 1992, again in New York, under the direction of Gregory Moshed, with Jessica Lange and Alec Baldwin. The play was also presented on ABC Television on 4 March 1984, with Ann-Margret and Treat Williams, and in CBS 'Playhouse 90' on 29 October 1995, with Jessica Lange and Alec Baldwin. A 2005 Broadway revival was directed by Edward Hall and produced by the Roundabout Theater Company, with John C. Reilly (Stanley), Amy Ryan (Stella) and Natasha Richardson (Blanche). In 2009 Pace University premiered an African-American direction directed by Steven McCasland. Unusually, it included the ghost of Blanche's dead husband, played by Sully Lennon.

British revivals

The London audience had to wait until 1974 for the first major revival of the play, directed by Edwin Sherwin, with Claire Bloom as Blanche and Martin Shaw as Stanley. Jack Tinker in the *Daily Mail* of 11 March 1974 had nothing but praise for Claire Bloom: 'Until now [Blanche's] steamy legend has belonged exclusively to Vivien Leigh. However, legends are only ever on loan and Bloom is here in London to prove how much mileage is left in the old *Streetcar*'. Similarly, Eric Johns in *Stage and Television Today* of 14 March 1974 declared 'No ghost will haunt Claire Bloom's Blanche'. John Walker in the *International Herald Tribune* of 23–4 March 1974 spoke of Bloom's Blanche as having 'all of Blanche's bitterness as well as vulnerability'.

KEY CONTEXT   A03

Do you think that present-day theatre audiences will judge *A Streetcar Named Desire* differently because of the recent resurgence of feminism?

In 2002 the National Theatre produced the play under the direction of Trevor Nunn, with Glenn Close as Blanche and Iain Glen as Stanley. The reviews were somewhat mixed; not surprisingly, in this age of the cult of celebrity, they concentrated on Glenn Close. Benedict Nightingale in *The Times* of 9 October 2002 spoke of 'a Blanche who … has moments of surprising radiance, wry insight, defensive rage … and a wincing, palpitating desperation'.

Less positively, Sheridan Morley in the *New Statesman* of 21 October 2002 remarked that 'Close [is] about as vulnerable as a Sherman tank' in 'this production which aches to be a musical'. Georgina Brown in the *Mail on Sunday* of 13 October 2002 saw Close's Blanche as 'not a threat … but an irritation, the thick-skinned sister-in-law from hell who hogs the bathroom'. In a more serious vein, for John Peter in the *Sunday Times* of 13 October 2002, Close's Blanche is a performer: 'Life is a succession of glamorous tableaux in which Blanche is the glamorous but anguished central figure … Close brings out … the difference between a melodramatic actress and a melodramatic character.'

London's Young Vic staged a major production of the play in 2014, directed by Benedict Andrews and starring Gillian Anderson (of *X-Files* fame) as Blanche and Ben Foster as Stanley (see photo). Critical response was on the whole very positive. The *Guardian*'s Susannah Clapp called Foster's Stanley 'a terrific tattooed bruiser who roars like a goaded bull' and called Anderson 'utterly compelling' (3 August 2014). She also showed how set design can make a point about a play: 'Magda Willi's in-the-round design makes it clear that no one has a monopoly on the truth.' The paper's Michael Billington gave a mixed response to the rotating stage, but commented that Anderson's Blanche captured 'both Blanche's airy pretensions to grandeur and her desolate loneliness' (29 July 2014).

A05 KEY INTERPRETATION

Michael Billington comments: '… the real test of any production of Williams's play is whether it allows you to see each character's point of view. If Blanche is simply played as a cracked Southern belle and Stanley as a coarse brute, the play descends into melodrama.'

A03

Progress booster: Productions over time

When writing about stage productions, it's important to consider how portrayals of the key characters have changed and developed. Over time, Stanley seems to be losing the machismo of the '*gaudy seed-bearer*' (Scene One, p. 13), the bullying pride. Blanche, on the other hand, has grown in assertiveness. Claire Bloom's performance of 1974 stressed the bitterness in Blanche, as well as her vulnerability. In the 2002 revival, the choice of Glenn Close as Blanche made a strong statement. Close, the vengeful 'bunny boiler' of the film *Fatal Attraction* (1987) is hardly Tennessee Williams's fluttering 'moth', though she won praise for her performance from some reviewers. Modern casting and interpretations can shed new light on the play, but at the same time, we may ask whether the influence of twenty-first century sexual politics on a play so firmly rooted in its period is justified, or unavoidable.

A feature of Gillian Anderson's 2014 performance was how well she captured Blanche's fragility from the outset, a habitual nervous laugh hinting at her awkwardness and vulnerability. Anderson makes Blanche's mental disintegration something that occurs gradually from Scene One, even if it speeds up after her rejection by Mitch, perhaps reflecting the more sensitive attitudes to mental illness today.

KEY INTERPRETATION

'Blanche is dangerous. She is destructive. She would soon have him and Stella fighting. He's got things the way he wants them around there and he does not want them upset by a phony, corrupt, sick, destructive woman. *This makes Stanley right!* Are we going into the era of Stanley? He may be practical and right. ... but what ... does it leave us?' (Elia Kazan, private director's notebook, cited in Cole, Toby & Krich Chinoy, Helen (eds), *Directors on Directing: A Source Book of the Modern Theatre*. 2nd rev., New York, Macmillan, 1988).

Contemporary approaches

Marxist approaches

According to a Marxist view, the plot, characters and themes of *Streetcar* express the socio-economic conditions and class struggles of 1940s America. The play's 'dialectical' conflicts and oppositions can be seen as leading towards their resolution. For example, a Marxist reading would view the play as a social drama working out the antagonism between the declining DuBois family and the newly assertive working class, represented by Stanley. It might see Stella's passivity as an acceptance of the rise of the working class. Similarly, it might see the Blanche–Stanley conflict as a doomed bourgeois attempt to resist working-class energy and realism.

Thus some critics have followed Elia Kazan's vision of Stanley as the hero defending his home and marriage against the threat represented by Blanche. This approach also relates to that of critics who see the play as depicting a clash between two cultural 'species', or in terms of Darwinian 'survival of the fittest', with Stanley being the survivor – the *'gaudy seed-bearer'* (Scene One, p. 13) whose actual seed is embodied in his new son, entering the world just as Blanche is forced out.

New Historicism

New Historicism, based on the ideas of Stephen Greenblatt, focuses on how a work is influenced by the context in which it was written, and on how interpretations are in turn influenced by the society in which a critic is writing. So, *A Streetcar Named Desire* reflects America in the 1940s. The play does not appear to be aiming at social commentary, yet its characters inevitably embody the values of the time. Hence Stanley, as a member of the urban working class, is proudly patriotic and convinced that he should be 'king' in his own home. Blanche, a product of the old Southern class system, believes in her innate superiority to Stanley. Stella is a loyal housewife who clears up after her husband. Even the fact that there were audiences for the play at all is a product of a period in which there was enough money and leisure to enjoy theatre, and sufficient interest in working-class characters like Stanley and Mitch to warrant writing a play about them.

New Historicism would also look at how our own social values influence our reading of the play. Hence we are probably more likely now to sympathise with Blanche than Stanley, and we are certainly unlikely to cheer when Stanley carries Blanche off to rape her – as some early audience members did.

Feminist readings

A feminist approach would focus on how the play reflects or challenges male-dominated social values. For example, Stella is subjugated to Stanley; Blanche is fired from one of the few occupations open to an intelligent, educated woman, and is portrayed as hysterical and mentally disturbed. A feminist approach might also examine how the text portrays men's moral double standards in relation to women, and women's sympathy, or lack of it, for other women. It might investigate female oppression implied in the author's technique. For example, Blanche is introduced by stage directions describing her appearance; with Stanley the focus is on his masculine energy.

A feminist might note that Stanley enjoys women but demands their obedience, whereas Mitch romanticises them. Stanley hits his pregnant wife, and later asserts his authority by smashing plates. A feminist interpretation would look at how Stella submits to Stanley, while Blanche tries to use her sexuality to resist him. It might also focus on the sisters' exclusion from the poker night, Blanche's breakdown as a response to a male-dominated world, and Stella's betrayal of her sister. The fact that Stella chooses to believe Stanley's version of events and not her sister's could be seen as history being 'written by the victors'.

Psychoanalytic criticism

Psychoanalytic criticism, based on the work of Sigmund Freud, might look at the characters as expressions of Williams's psyche, or at the psychology of the characters. This approach tends to see conflicts as being within or between individuals, rather than as social (as in a Marxist approach). Freud investigated how the unconscious expresses itself in dream symbolism, and in emotional and sexual drives. Hence the play's symbols and imagery would be examples of unconscious impulses at work. A Freudian approach would highlight the play's preoccupation with sexual desire and fear of death. One based more on the work of Freud's disciple Carl Jung might see characters as representing archetypes in the 'collective unconscious' – which is shared with other human beings, or as repressed aspects of the self. Hence Stanley and Blanche might be seen as polarised male and female forces, each drawn to, but failing to understand, the other.

A psychoanalytical reading might examine Williams's homosexuality and guilt, and how the play embodies the psychic drives of Eros (sex and love) and Thanatos (death), symbolised by the streetcars named 'Desire' and 'Cemeteries', and played out in Blanche taking refuge from her fear of death in promiscuity, and expressing her guilt in audio-hallucinations and frequent bathing. A Jungian interpretation might see Blanche as a 'negative anima' figure representing an imagined threat to men, the anima being the repressed or undeveloped female aspect of the male psyche. Her ironic reference to 'The Tarantula Arms' (Scene Nine, p. 87) expresses this.

Structuralism

A structuralist interpretation, based on the theories of Ferdinand de Saussure, might focus on the play's structure and how this relates to other plays. Thus it would ask how far the play conforms to the genre of tragedy. It would also look at intertextuality – how it draws on and relates to other texts, for example in its references to poetry and popular songs. Elements of structuralism are linked closely to narrative theories, especially in relation to archetypes and myths, in work developed by critics such as Northrop Frye.

Structuralists would also consider the play's division into into eleven short scenes, all set in the Kowalski apartment, as well as its narrative arc: an 'initiating incident', which happens before the start of the play, when Blanche is fired; a period of 'rising action' consisting of 'successes and reverses'; a 'crisis' – the failed birthday party; a 'climax' – the rape; and then the 'falling action' of the final scene. The play might be seen as either a tragedy, like Ibsen's *Hedda Gabler*, or a melodrama, like Frederick Hazleton's *Sweeney Todd, the Barber of Fleet Street* (1865).

A05 KEY INTERPRETATION

Mary Ann Corrigan sees the Blanche–Stanley struggle as a dramatisation of what is going on inside Blanche's head: 'the external events of the play, while actually occurring, serve as a metaphor for Blanche's internal conflict' ('Realism and Theatricalism in *A Streetcar Named Desire*', *Modern Drama*, 19 (Dec. 1976), 385–96).

A05 KEY INTERPRETATION

'... the play is structured on the basis of the oppositions past/present and paradise lost/present chaos; the characters are defined in terms of the way they relate to time, or, in other words, by their ability or lack of ability to accept or adapt to the historical process.' (Ana Lucia Almeida Gazolla, '*A Streetcar Named Desire*: Myth, Ritual, and Ideology,' in Don Harkness (ed.), *Ritual in the United States: Acts and Representations*, Tampa, FL, American Studies, 1985, 23–27.)

PROGRESS CHECK

Section One: Check your understanding

These short tasks will help you to evaluate your knowledge and skills level in this particular area.

1. What real settings are used in *A Streetcar Named Desire*?
2. How is the American Civil War relevant to the play?
3. How is the Second World War relevant to the play?
4. What factors in Williams's personal life find their way into the play?
5. Who directed the first film version of the play, and in what key way does its ending differ from the play?
6. Note down two or three ways in which the play has been criticised in performance.
7. What play by Chekhov can be compared with *A Streetcar Named Desire*, and how?
8. List three ways in which *The Duchess of Malfi* is like *A Streetcar Named Desire*.
9. Name one way in which the play might be interpreted according to psychoanalytical theory.
10. What might a feminist critique of the play focus on?

Section Two: Working towards the exam

Choose one of the following three tasks, which require longer, more developed answers.

1. How does Williams's use of setting contribute to the dramatic force of the play?
2. In what senses is *A Streetcar Named Desire* a play rooted in the 1940s?
3. On what issues might a feminist approach to the play focus?

PROGRESS BOOSTER **A01**

For each of the Section Two tasks, read the question carefully, select the key areas you need to address, and plan an essay of six to seven points. Write a first draft, giving yourself an hour to do so. Make sure you include supporting evidence for each point, including quotations.

Progress check (Rate your understanding on a level of 1 – low, to 5 – high)	1	2	3	4	5
The significance of setting in the play					
How the play relates to its historical and literary context					
The overall structure of the play and how events are linked					
The play's reception by reviewers and how this developed					
The different critical approaches to the play (such as 'New historicism')					

ASSESSMENT FOCUS

How will you be assessed?

Each particular exam board and exam paper will be slightly different, so make sure you check with your teacher exactly which Assessment Objectives you need to focus on. You are likely to get more marks for Assessment Objectives 1, 2 and 3, but this does not mean you should discount 4 or 5.

What do the AOs actually mean?

	Assessment Objective	Meaning
AO1	Articulate informed, personal and creative responses to literary texts, using associated concepts and terminology, and coherent, accurate written expression.	You write about texts in accurate, clear and precise ways so that what you have to say is clear to the marker. You use literary terms (e.g. **'protagonist'**) or refer to concepts (e.g. **'tragic flaw'**) in relevant places. You do not simply repeat what you have read or been told, but express your own ideas based on in-depth knowledge of the text and related issues.
AO2	Analyse ways in which meanings are shaped in literary texts.	You are able to explain in detail how the specific techniques and methods used by Tennessee Williams (e.g. recurrent **symbols** or **motifs**) influence and affect the reader's response.
AO3	Demonstrate understanding of the significance and influence of the contexts in which literary texts are written and received.	You can explain how the play might reflect the social, historical, political or personal backgrounds of Williams or the time when it was written. You also consider how the play might have been received differently over time by audiences and readers.
AO4	Explore connections across literary texts.	You are able to explain links between the play and other texts, perhaps of a similar genre, or with similar concerns, or viewed from a similar perspective (e.g. feminist).
AO5	Explore literary texts informed by different interpretations.	You understand how the play can be viewed in different ways, and are able to write about these debates, forming your own opinion. For example, how a critic might view Blanche as a symbol of the decaying 'plantation' culture of the South, while another might see her as a tragically doomed individual.

What does this mean for your revision?

Whether you are following an A Level or AS course, use the right-hand column above as a way of measuring how confidently you can respond to questions related to these issues. Depending on your level of confidence, you can focus your revision on those aspects you feel need most attention. Remember, throughout these Notes, the AOs are highlighted, so you can flick through and check them in that way.

However, two key things now need to be done:

- First, you need to understand how attainment in each of these AOs differs – for example, between writing something that is satisfactory, and something that is outstanding. The grid on page 82 will help in this regard.

- Second, you need to know how to decode questions and plan responses in the exam, so that you know how to address the key AOs. The work from page 83 onwards will help you here.

It is very important to understand how you can make progress. The following tables, while not comprehensive, should give you some idea of different levels of attainment.

Features of **mid-level** responses: the following examples relate to the idea of betrayal.

	Features	Examples
AO1	You use critical vocabulary and your arguments are relevant to the task, with clear expression. You show detailed knowledge of the text.	*Williams demonstrates the terrible consequences of betrayal in 'A Streetcar Named Desire'. Blanche's instability is caused at least partly by her sense of guilt for having caused her husband's suicide, but it can be argued that Stella is ultimately responsible for Blanche's mental breakdown by choosing to believe Stanley's version of events.*
AO2	You show straightforward understanding of how form, structure and language shape meanings.	*Williams carefully manages the action of the plot so that there is no let-up in the pace and tension, once Mitch has been told about Blanche's promiscuity. For example, Williams's organisation of events in Scenes Seven to Ten creates a sense of drama and claustrophobia.*
AO3	You can write about a range of contextual factors and make some relevant links with the task or text.	*There was still great stigma attached to divorce and single parenthood in 1940s America, and little social welfare, so it comes as no surprise that Stella chooses to believe her husband rather than to believe Blanche's rape claim and leave him.*
AO4	You consider straightforward connections between texts and write about them clearly and relevantly to the task.	*In 'Much Ado About Nothing' Shakespeare presents Claudio as a man who is too willing to believe false accusations about his fiancée Hero, and who therefore shames her. In 'A Streetcar Named Desire' Mitch is reluctant to believe accusations against Blanche that turn out to be true. In both cases it is a woman's reputation that is at stake.*
AO5	You tackle the debate in a clear, logical way, showing understanding of different interpretations.	*We could see Stanley as the hero of the play, as he was shown in the first Broadway production. In this case, he is justified in defending his marriage against the intruder – Blanche. Alternatively, we can see him as a brutal rapist who betrays his wife.*

Features of a **high-level response**: these examples relate to a task on the theme of desire and fate.

	Features	Examples
AO1	You are perceptive, and assured in your argument in relation to the task. You make fluent, confident use of literary concepts and terms.	*Williams shows there is a tragic imperative that drives Blanche relentlessly towards her fate. This is coherent with classical notions of inevitability – a sense that events conspire against her to the point that her fall can be seen as ordained from the moment she arrives in Elysian Fields.*
AO2	You explore and analyse key aspects of form, structure and language and evaluate perceptively how they shape meanings.	*Williams makes effective use of symbolism. Blanche takes a 'streetcar named Desire' and changes for one heading to 'Cemeteries', showing that what she metaphorically terms the 'rattle-trap streetcar' of sexual desire leads inevitably to death. It is homosexual desire that leads to her husband's suicide, which haunts her.*
AO3	You show detailed and relevant understanding of how contextual factors link to the text or task.	*If Blanche represents the decaying world of the plantation families of the slave-owning American South, which had never recovered economically from the Civil War, then Stanley embodies the USA that emerged victorious from the Second World War.*
AO4	You show a detailed and perceptive understanding of issues raised through connections between texts. You have a range of excellent supportive references.	*Shakespeare's Macbeth achieves the status of tragic hero, despite his appalling crimes, because he accepts responsibility for his fate. His wife cannot be called a tragic heroine, because she is mentally disturbed. Similarly, while Stanley creates his own fate through self-belief, Blanche cannot become truly tragic because she cannot even comprehend her own fate, and so cannot accept it.*
AO5	You use your knowledge of critical debates, and possible perspectives on an issue to write fluently about how the text might be interpreted.	*One school of thought sees the play as an expression of Darwinian natural selection, with Stanley motivated by desire, and simply taking what he wants because he can. This kind of social determinism could be seen as a modern-day version of the genre conventions of tragedy, by which Blanche is doomed by fate.*

HOW TO WRITE HIGH-QUALITY RESPONSES

The quality of your writing – how you express your ideas – is vital for getting a higher grade, and **AO1** and **AO2** are specifically about **how** you respond.

Five key areas

1. The structure of your answer/essay

> **EXAMINER'S TIP**
>
> AO1 and AO2 are equally important in AS and A Level responses.

- First, get **straight to the point in your opening paragraph.** Use a sharp, direct first sentence that deals with a key aspect and then follow up with evidence or a detailed reference.
- **Put forward an argument or point of view** (you won't **always** be able to challenge or take issue with the essay question, but generally, where you can, you are more likely to write in an interesting way).
- **Signpost your ideas** with connectives and references which help the essay flow. Aim to present an overall argument or conceptual response to the task, not a series of unconnected points.
- **Don't repeat points already made,** not even in the conclusion, unless you have something new to add.

Aiming high: Effective opening paragraphs

Let's imagine you have been asked about the following question:

'Tragedy is concerned with the acceptance of fate.' Examine this view of *A Streetcar Named Desire*.

> Gets straight to the point

In 'Streetcar', the importance of fate is implicit in the symbolism of the title, in which fate is the streetcar running on its unbending tramlines, and desire is what propels it. Against this concept, Williams sets the idea of free will, expressed in Blanche's moment of greatest hope that she can get off the streetcar and make a new life with Mitch: 'Sometimes – there's God – so quickly!'

> Sets up some interesting ideas that will be tackled in subsequent paragraphs

2. Use of titles, names, etc.

This is a simple, but important, tip to stay on the right side of the examiners.

- Make sure that you spell correctly the titles of texts, authors and so on. Present them correctly too, with quotation marks and capitals as appropriate. For example, *In Scene One of 'A Streetcar Named Desire …'*
- Use a shortened version of the title to save time, i.e. *Streetcar*.
- Use the term 'text' or 'play', rather than 'book' or 'story'. If you use the word 'story', the examiner may think you mean the plot/action rather than the 'text' as a whole.

3. Effective quotations

Do not 'bolt on' quotations to the points you make. You will get some marks for including them, but examiners will not find your writing very fluent.

The best quotations are:

- Relevant and not too long (you are going to have to memorise them, so that will help you select shorter ones!)
- Integrated into your argument/sentence
- Linked to effect and implications

Aiming high: Effective use of quotations

Here is an example of an effective use of a quotation about jealousy in the play:

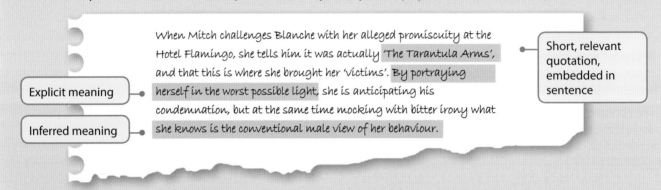

When Mitch challenges Blanche with her alleged promiscuity at the Hotel Flamingo, she tells him it was actually 'The Tarantula Arms', and that this is where she brought her 'victims'. By portraying herself in the worst possible light, she is anticipating his condemnation, but at the same time mocking with bitter irony what she knows is the conventional male view of her behaviour.

Explicit meaning

Inferred meaning

Short, relevant quotation, embedded in sentence

Remember – quotations can also be one or two single words or phrases embedded in a sentence to build a picture or explanation, or they can be longer ones that are explored and picked apart.

4. Techniques and terminology

By all means mention literary terms, techniques, conventions, critical theories or people (for example, 'paradox', 'archetype', 'feminism' or 'Elia Kazan') **but** make sure that you:

- Understand what they mean, or to whom they refer
- Are able to link them to what you're saying
- Spell them correctly

5. General writing skills

Try to write in a way that sounds professional and uses standard English. This does not mean that your writing will lack personality – just that it will be authoritative.

- Avoid colloquial or everyday expressions such as 'got', 'gotten', 'alright', 'OK' and so on.
- Use terms such as 'convey', 'suggest', 'imply', 'infer' to explain the writer's methods.
- Refer to 'we' when discussing the audience/reader.
- Avoid assertions and generalisations; don't just state a general point of view ('Stanley is a typical villain because he's evil'), but analyse closely with clear evidence and textual detail.

Note the approach here in the choice of vocabulary and awareness of the effect:

> EXAMINER'S TIP
>
> It's important to remember that *A Streetcar Named Desire* is a text created by Tennessee Williams – thinking about the choices Williams makes with language and plotting will not only alert you to his methods as a playwright but also his intentions, i.e. the effect he seeks to create.

Stanley has some of the typical qualities of the melodramatic villain. For example, he moves 'stealthily' to conceal the fact that he has eavesdropped on Blanche's condemnation of his 'sub-human' nature, so that he can plot his revenge. He is able to disguise his resentment behind a facade of casual good humour.

RESPONDING TO A GENERAL QUESTION ABOUT THE WHOLE TEXT

You may be asked to write about a specific aspect of *A Streetcar Named Desire*. This might be a key issue or idea, or on the way Williams uses language. For example, a 'key idea' question:

> **Explore how social class is presented in *A Streetcar Named Desire*. You must relate your discussion to relevant contextual factors.**

Or it might be a question related to language, structure or something else that is noteworthy in the text:

> **Explore the role of deception in the action of *A Streetcar Named Desire*, and how it is presented.**

Let us take the first question. If you are tackling that question, you need to:

- Focus on the importance of class differences in the play, such as the different values of the Kowalski and DuBois families.
- Explain *how* Williams presents or organises ideas about this. For example, look at the speech and imagery of Stanley and Blanche, at their attitudes, and at their preferred leisure activities – such as bowling and reading poetry.
- Look at the whole text, not just one scene or character.
- Consider context and critical ideas – this means looking at the background of the DuBois family and at Stanley's pride in his unrefined manners and tastes, and at how far we should interpret Blanche and Stanley as individuals involved in a personal struggle, and how far we should see them as class representatives.

Structuring your response

You need a clear, logical plan, but it will be impossible to write about every aspect or section of the play. Start by noting down five or six key ideas:

A:	Blanche is a member of a declining 'plantation' family, like many who lost much of their wealth after the defeat of the South in the Civil War; Stanley is a working-class man, of Polish family background but proud to be American.
B:	Stella has happily compromised her old family values in the interests of passion and raising a family. This could be seen as the way forward for the South, and families like the DuBois.
C:	Members of different classes in the play speak and behave differently, revealing fundamental differences in values.
D:	It could be that Blanche speaks for Williams when she says 'Don't hang back with the brutes', and that the play is about the tragedy of brute masculinity overcoming tenderer feelings.
E:	Finally, it is about basic misunderstandings between social classes, but also between men and women. Is it an appeal for understanding?

Then decide the most effective order for your points (e.g. C, A, B, D, E), and draw in supporting evidence *and* references to context or critical ideas. Turn to the next page for an example of a developed plan.

EXAMINER'S TIP

Answer the question set, not the question you'd like to have been asked. Examiners say that often students will be set a question on one character (for example, Stella) but end up writing almost as much about another (such as Blanche). Or they write about one aspect of the question (for example, 'fate') but ignore another (such as 'free will'). **Stick to the question**, and answer **all parts of it**.

Example of a developed plan for the question below:

> **Explore how social class is presented in *A Streetcar Named Desire*. You must relate your discussion to relevant contextual factors.**

Introduction: *Williams raises issues of social class very early in the play, showing Blanche's insensitive snubbing of the well-meaning but lower-class Eunice, and more subtly in the first line Stella speaks to Stanley: 'Don't holler at me like that.'*

Paragraph 1 (point C, say): *Blanche often uses fanciful imagery, as one might expect of someone who until recently was an English teacher. For example, she pictures Stanley and his poker-playing friends as cavemen. Later, she talks about her soldier lovers being gathered up 'like daisies'.*

Paragraph 2 (expand on point C): *Stanley, on the other hand, uses more down-to-earth imagery – the language of the street or factory. For example, life to him is a 'rat-race'. When he is more colourful, it is only to be insulting, as when he refers to Blanche's outfit as a 'worn-out Mardi Gras outfit, rented for fifty cents from some rag-picker'. His language is used competitively and assertively, whereas Blanche often seems to use language to entertain herself.*

Paragraph 3 (change direction, now look at Point A, say): *As a member of a once-wealthy family, Blanche finds it natural to be waited on, even by her own sister.*

… and so on.

For your conclusion: use a compelling way to finish, perhaps repeating words from the question. For example, you might end with a final point, but adding a last clause to clarify what you think is key to the answer:

> *In the final scene of the play, Williams seems to be telling us that it is inevitable that the brutish and powerful in society will triumph over the weak and sensitive, but it may be that hope lies in Stella, who represents a more benevolent compromise between fanciful weakness and brutishness.*

You could also end with a new quotation or aspect that is slightly different from your main point:

> *Williams reportedly said that the true meaning of 'A Streetcar Named Desire' was 'You had better look out or the apes will take over.' Indeed it seems hard to believe that he wanted to leave us with the conviction that a world in which a dominant man can get away with rape is a better one than that of the decaying South.*

Or, you could even combine these two types of conclusion.

RESPONDING TO A STATEMENT, VIEWPOINT OR QUOTATION

You may come across questions which include a statement, quotation or viewpoint that offers a particular interpretation of the text. These might be in relation to the whole text or with regard to a specific extract, and may deal with character or key ideas. For example:

> **'This is essentially a play about misunderstanding, not conflicting goals.' Examine this view of *A Streetcar Named Desire*.**

Or:

> **Examine the view that *A Streetcar Named Desire* fails because Blanche is unable to achieve true tragic dignity.**

The key thing to remember is that you are being asked to **respond to a particular perspective or critical view of the text** – in other words, to come up with **your own** 'take' on the idea or viewpoint in the task.

Key skills required

The table below provides help and advice on answering the first question above.

Skill	Means?	How do I achieve this?
To consider different interpretations	There will be more than one way of looking at the given question. For example, critics might be divided about how far Stanley's treatment of Blanche is justified.	Show you have considered these different interpretations in your answer through the way you juxtapose or weigh up ideas. For example: *We could see Stanley's behaviour as primarily motivated by a desire to protect his home and marriage, especially now that a baby is on the way. At the same time, Blanche's self-absorbed insensitivity gives him ample cause for resentment, and to seek revenge.*
To write with a clear, personal voice	Your own 'take' on the question is made obvious to the examiner. You are not just repeating other people's ideas, but offering what **you** think.	Although you may mention different perspectives on the task, you should settle on your own view. Use language that shows careful, but confident, consideration. For example: *Although Constance Drake has called 'Streetcar' a pessimistic play in which modern man destroys 'the tender aspects of love', I see considerable optimism in the overcoming of social barriers in the Kowalski marriage.*
To construct a coherent argument	The examiner can follow your train of thought so that your own viewpoint is clear to him or her.	Write in clear paragraphs that deal logically with different aspects of the question. Support what you say with well-selected and relevant evidence. Use a range of connectives to help 'signpost' your argument. For example: *We might say that Blanche misleads Mitch for her own ends. However, as she tells him, she merely gives people what they want. Moreover, his attempts to have sex with her show his own double standards.*

Responding to a 'viewpoint' question

On the next page you will find advice on answering this type of question, step-by-step.

Let us look at another question:

> **'In *A Streetcar Named Desire* Stella is a stereotype of female passivity.' To what extent do you agree with this view of Williams's dramatic presentation of Stella?**

Stage 1: Decode the question

Underline/highlight the key words, and make sure you understand what the statement, quote or viewpoint is saying. In this case:

'stereotype of female passivity' means: *a female character who uncomplainingly accepts her role in a male-dominated world*

'dramatic presentation of Stella' means: *how Williams uses dialogue, actions and stage directions to convey a concept of Stella as a character*

'To what extent' *invites you to weigh up the arguments – not simply agree or disagree*

So, you are being asked how far the presentation of Stella shows her as simply doing as she is told by Stanley, and how far it shows her as acting independently.

Stage 2: Decide how to structure your answer

Pick out the key points you wish to make, and decide on the order that you will present them in. Keep this basic plan to hand while you write your response.

Stage 3: Write your response

Begin by paraphrasing or restating the issue, and then immediately suggesting a useful avenue to explore. Do not just repeat what the question says or simply say what you are going to do in the rest of the introductory paragraph. Get straight to the point. For example:

Paragraph 1:

Stanley is at the centre of Stella's world, as she makes clear when she tells Blanche that she 'can hardly stand it when he is away for a night' (Scene One). However, the idea that she must be seen, ultimately, as someone who is unable or unwilling to act independently is interesting given that her first words to Stanley in the play are 'Don't holler at me like that.'

I would argue that far from being passive, Stella accommodates Stanley's dominant nature because she loves him and feels passion for him, but that she also stands up to him.

Then proceed to set out the different arguments or perspectives, including your own. This might be done by dealing with specific aspects or elements of the play one by one. Consider giving one or two paragraphs to explore each aspect in turn. Discuss the strengths and weaknesses in each particular point of view. For example:

Paragraph 2: first aspect:

To explore this idea, we need to first of all look at …

It is clear from this that …/A strength of this argument is …

However, I believe this suggests that …/A weakness in this perspective is …

Paragraph 3: a new focus or aspect:

Turning our attention to … it could be said that …

Paragraphs 4, 5, etc.: develop the argument, building a convincing set of points.

Last paragraph: end with a statement of your view, without listing all the points made.

RESPONDING TO A COMPARISON OR LINKED TEXT QUESTION

If you are following the WJEC/Eduqas specification, you will be asked to compare *A Streetcar Named Desire* with *The Duchess of Malfi* by John Webster.

Linking or comparison questions might relate to a particular theme or idea, such as 'contexts' – for example:

> **How far would you agree that both Webster and Williams create heroines who arouse our pity and command our respect in *The Duchess of Malfi* and *A Streetcar Named Desire*?**

Or:

> **'What strikes us most is the treachery faced by women.' In the light of this statement, explore connections between *The Duchess of Malfi* and *A Streetcar Named Desire*.**

You will need to **evaluate** the issue or statement and have an **open-minded approach**. The best answers suggest meanings and interpretations (plural):

- For example, in relation to the first question: do you agree that the heroines of both texts arouse pity and respect? Is the balance of the two different in the two texts? Why? How?
- What are the different ways that this question or these aspects can be read or viewed?
- What evidence is there in each text for this perspective? How can you present it in a thoughtful, reflective way?
- What are the points of similarity and difference?

Express **original or creative approaches** fluently:

- This isn't about coming up with entirely new ideas, but you need to show that you're actively engaged with thinking about the question, not just reeling off things you have learned.
- **Synthesise** your ideas – pull ideas and points together to create something fresh.
- This is a linking/comparison response, so ensure that you guide your reader through your ideas logically, clearly and with professional language.

Know *what* **to compare/contrast**: the writer's methods – **form, structure and language** – will **always** be central to your response. Consider:

- Authorial perspective revealed in stage directions, the distinctive things about the play form that can be compared/contrasted (e.g. the influence of characters' entrances and exits, division of the action into scenes, etc.)
- Different characteristic use of language (lengths of sentences, formal/informal style, dialect, accent, balance of dialogue and monologue or stage directions)
- Variety of symbols, images, motifs (how they represent concerns of author/time; what they are and how and where they appear; how they link to critical perspectives; their purposes, effects and impact on the drama)
- Shared or differing approaches (to what extent do Williams and Webster conform to/challenge/subvert approaches to writing about women)

EXAMINER'S TIP

Remember that in order to score highly in your answer you will also need to discuss what the critics say (AO5) and consider relevant cultural or contextual factors (AO3).

Writing your response

The depth of your answer will depend on how much you have to write, but the key will be to explore in detail, and link between, ideas and texts. To use the earlier example:

> How far do you agree that both Webster and Williams create heroines who arouse our pity and command our respect in *The Duchess of Malfi* and *A Streetcar Named Desire*?

EXAMINER'S TIP

You should comment concisely, professionally and thoughtfully and present a range of viewpoints. Try using modal verbs such as 'would', 'could', 'might', 'may' to clarify your own interpretation.

Introduction to your response

- Discuss quickly what 'arouse our pity and command our respect' means, and how well this applies to *A Streetcar Named Desire* and *The Duchess of Malfi*.
- Mention in support the key relationships that exist in both plays.
- You could begin with a powerful quotation to launch into your response. For example:

'In some kinds of people some tenderer feelings have had some little beginning!' Blanche pleads, in an attempt to make Stella see that she cannot remain with a man who is 'sub-human'. We know from her references to Poe, Whitman and Hawthorne, and her sensitive attachment to the memory of her husband, that Blanche is one of these people. This makes her worthy of our respect, but it also makes her extremely vulnerable in a world dominated by men like Stanley.

Main body of your response

- **Point 1:** start with one way in which Blanche earns our respect in *A Streetcar Named Desire*: what this implies about 1940s American society, why this was/was not 'interesting' for audiences at the time, and now. How might we interpret her behaviour differently through time? What do the critics say? Are there contextual/cultural factors to consider?
- **Point 2:** now cover a new factor or aspect through comparison or contrast of this characteristic for which we respect Blanche with another in *The Duchess of Malfi*. For example, how is a capacity for independent thinking presented differently or similarly by Webster according to language, form, structures used; why was this done in this way; how does it reflect the writer's interests? What do the critics say? Are there contextual factors?
- **Points 3, 4, 5, etc.:** address a range of other factors and aspects, for example other ways in which the heroine earns our respect or arouses our pity in either *A Streetcar Named Desire* or in both *A Streetcar Named Desire* and *The Duchess of Malfi*. What different ways do you respond to these (with more empathy, greater criticism, less interest) – and why?

Blanche manages to inspire both our pity and our respect in equal measure in Scene Nine, which could be regarded as the crisis point of the play – when Blanche stands to gain or lose most. We cannot help but pity her as her initial hope on Mitch's arrival turns to reluctant acceptance that she can no longer hold out against his accusation that she has not been 'straight' with him about her past. Her brave attempts to make light of the situation, in jokes such as 'So utterly uncavalier!' are pitiful because of Williams's use of dramatic irony. We know from Scene Eight that Stanley has told Mitch about Blanche's life at the Hotel Flamingo, and that this is the reason for his uncouth appearance and surly manner.

Conclusion

- Synthesise elements of what you have said into a final paragraph that leaves the reader/examiner with the sense that you have engaged with this task and the texts.

In 'The Duchess of Malfi', the Duchess is a strong woman who defies her brothers' wishes. She asserts her free will not only by remarrying, but by choosing a man of lower status, Antonio. When discovered she stands up to Ferdinand as Blanche attempts to do with Stanley. Ferdinand tries to drive the Duchess mad, but ultimately she dies accepting her fate with tragic dignity. Blanche, on the other hand, can be pitied at the end of 'Streetcar' but is too mentally disturbed to understand her fate.

WRITING ABOUT CONTEXTS

Depending on the particular course you are following, you may need to focus on aspects of context that are relevant to the general area you are being asked to explore. In this regard, there are some key things to remember:

Assessment Objective 3 asks you to 'demonstrate understanding of the significance and influence of the contexts in which literary texts are written and received'. This can mean:

- How the events, settings, politics and so on of the time when the text was written influenced the writer or help us to understand the play's themes or concerns. For example, to what extent Williams might have been influenced by his society's attitudes towards class and gender

Or:

- How events, settings, politics and so on of the time when the text is read or seen influence how it is understood. For example, would modern audiences brought up in a world of greater class and gender equality respond differently to the Kowalski marriage than a 1940s audience?

You might find the following table helpful for thinking about how particular aspects of the time in which the play was written contribute to our understanding now of the play and its themes – for example, in relation to the question on page 90.

Political	Literary	Philosophical
The South's impoverishment by the Civil War. The play's first performance coming three years after American victory in the Second World War.	The idea of Southern Gothic, featuring elements of the grotesque and melodrama. Edgar Allan Poe (mentioned by Blanche), Strindberg and Ibsen. The conventions of certain types of tragedy and how the play conforms to or subverts them.	Nietzsche's ideas about the Superman, mistakenly interpreted by some as a justification of eugenics. Existentialism: Stanley could be seen as a man who creates his own meaning by believing in his own luck.
Scientific	**Cultural**	**Social**
Darwinian beliefs about the survival of the fittest: Stanley could be seen as the arch-survivor. He survives the war and he triumphs over Blanche. He also fathers a child, passing on his own genes.	Attitudes towards 'old' money and immigration; the 'melting pot' vision of a United States and the extent to which this was idealised. The influence of World War Two as a social leveller.	Attitudes towards women, and towards homosexuality. Homosexuality was still illegal in most states of the USA when the play was written.

Aiming high: Making context relevant

It is very important that you do not approach context as something to be 'bolted on' to what you say. You must make fluent links between contextual knowledge and the focus of the task. For example, **don't** just write:

In the 1940s, the Southern states had still not entirely recovered economically from the Civil War that ended in 1865. Many once-wealthy families were in decline, and old plantations had been broken up. In 1945 the US had recently been victorious in the Second World War. It was a time of increasing economic growth and leisure.

Do write:

Blanche and Stella DuBois are members of the old plantation- and slave-owning elite that had never recovered from the Civil War that ended in 1865. Blanche herself shows the snobbishness of her background in her attitude towards Eunice, snubbing her in both Scene One and Scene Two. She also demonstrates class prejudice – and even racial prejudice – against Stanley, whom she refers to as 'sub-human' and a 'Polack'. Stanley, for his part, fought for the USA in the Second World War, and shows fierce patriotism, and a self-belief that may stem in part from his survival against the odds in the war.

USING CRITICAL INTERPRETATIONS AND PERSPECTIVES

What is a critical interpretation?

The particular way a text is viewed or understood can be called an interpretation, and can be made by literary critics (specialists in studying literary texts), reviewers or everyday readers and students. Looking at the text from a critical perspective does not necessarily mean finding what is wrong with it or what you object to, but is more about taking a position on particular elements of the text, or on what others say about it. For example:

1. Notions of 'character'

- Is the character an 'archetype' (a specific type of character with common features)? (For example, Stanley could be seen as an archetypal villain in melodrama, and Blanche as an archetypal victim.
- Does the character personify, symbolise or represent a specific idea or **trope** (the noble heroine brought down by a fatal flaw; how power preys on weakness)?
- Is the character modern, universal, of his/her time, historically accurate, etc.? (For example, is Stanley the embodiment of Darwinian ideas of natural selection or, like many modern villains, driven by selfish, petty motives?)

2. Ideas and issues

What the play tells us about particular ideas or issues and how we interpret these.

For example:

- Ideas about natural selection, e.g. the belief that society benefits if people like Stanley are allowed to compete without restraint
- The role of men/women in society and within marriage
- What **tragedy** means to 1940s and modern audiences
- Moral and social attitudes towards sexuality

3. Links and contexts

How the play links with, follows or pre-echoes other texts, ideas. For example:

- Its influence culturally, historically and socially. Do we see echoes of the characters or genres in other texts? How similar to other heroines is Blanche and why? Does her characterisation share features with the plays of Ibsen and Strindberg, or David Mamet, for example?
- How its language links to other texts or modes, such as religious works, myth, legend, etc.

KEY INTERPRETATION **A05**

Guardian theatre critic Michael Billington said of Ben Foster's performance: 'There is something dangerous about this sweaty, tattooed, close-cropped Stanley who has recently been discharged from the military and who has not lost his combative instinct. At the same time, you understand his refusal to be patronised and insulted by his affected sister-in-law.'

4. Genre and dramatic structure

How the play is constructed and how Williams makes his narrative.

- Does it follow a particular dramatic convention?
- What is the function of specific events, characters, theatrical devices, staging, etc., in relation to narrative?
- What are the specific moments of tension, conflict, crisis and **denouement** – and do we agree on what they are?

5. Audience and critical reaction

How the play works on an audience or reader, and whether this changes over time and in different contexts. Also, how different types of reader have responded, from reviewers, to actors and directors, to academics and researchers. For example:

- How far do readers or audiences empathise with, feel distance from, judge and/or evaluate the events and characters?
- What ideas do they find compelling and convincing, or lacking in truth and impact?
- How far do they see the play as unique and modern, part of a tradition or carrying echoes of other works and ideas?

Writing about critical perspectives

The important thing to remember is that **you** are a critic too. Your job is to evaluate what a critic or school of criticism has said about the elements above, arrive at your own conclusions, and also express your own ideas.

In essence, you need to: **consider** the views of others, **synthesise** them, then decide on **your perspective**. For example:

Explain the viewpoints

Critical view A about Stanley and Blanche:

> *Elia Kazan comments, 'Blanche is dangerous. She is destructive.' Under his direction, Blanche was an unstable woman who had entered and threatened the security of a different world, and who was finally cast out, allowing that world to survive.*

Critical view B about the same aspect:

> *As interpreted by Harold Clurman, Blanche is a delicate and sensitive woman pushed into insanity by a brutish environment presided over by chief ape-man Stanley Kowalski.*

Then synthesise and add your perspective

> *Blanche is certainly unbalanced from the start of the play, as she admits to Stella when she says she is 'not very well' and cannot 'be alone'. The danger she represents, as interpreted by Elia Kazan's interpretation of her character, is made apparent in her 'I took the blows' speech, in which she goes on the attack to pre-empt any criticism from Stella. Even more, she makes a serious attempt to persuade Stella to leave the father of her unborn baby because he is 'sub-human'. On the other hand, Blanche's undoubted sensitivity is seen in her exchanges with Mitch, and especially in her sympathy for his impending bereavement. She is a dangerously disruptive force, but she still deserves our compassion as a woman traumatised by the suicide of her husband and victimised by male-dominated society.*

A05 KEY INTERPRETATION

In *The Guardian* theatre critic Susannah Clapp said: 'Ben Foster's Stanley is a terrific tattooed bruiser who roars like a goaded bull. He is, as he should be, both bullying – 'I'm king around here' – and magnetic.'

ANNOTATED SAMPLE ANSWERS

Below are extracts from three sample answers at different levels to the same task/question. Bear in mind that these responses may not correspond exactly to the style of question you might face, but they will give a broad indication of some of the key skills required.

> **Question: 'Men in *A Streetcar Named Desire* are mostly despicable; it is the women who show nobility of character.' How far do you agree with this view?**

Candidate 1

A01 Needs explanation

A04 Awareness of genre and citical views

I agree with this view. After all, Blanche is the play's tragic heroine. Some critics say that she only achieves this status by the end, but early on she at least deserves our sympathy. Right at the start a stage direction says she is like a 'moth', because she is vulnerable and fluttery. She also tells Stella in Scene One that 'you must have noticed – I'm not very well …' She looks frightened as she says this, which makes us sympathetic. She has had a tough time in her past, with her husband killing himself because he was gay and she found out, so she feels guilty. When she tells Mitch this he is sympathetic and so are we. She also hints to Stella that she has had to give herself to men when she says 'soft people have got to court the favour of hard ones' (Scene Five). What this means is clearer in Scene Eight when she says she has had sex with many men, including soldiers, in the Hotel Tarantula. These days we might not be bothered about this but Mitch obviously is.

A01 Begins to make a valid point but needs more explanation

A03 Reference to context is vague and needs elaboration

A01 Unclear or misunderstood

A01 Slips into retelling

Blanche fails to get Mitch to marry her, and then in Scene Ten gets drunk and starts to lose her mind. This leads to the fight with Stanley when she tries to defend herself with a broken bottle, and then to the rape which happens offstage (like in a Greek tragedy) but is the terrible climax of the play. At the end she is fantasising about Shep Huntleigh and dying at sea from eating a grape. It is horrible when the Doctor and Nurse come for her, and most people would surely sympathise.

A04 Basic awareness of genre

A02 Simple analysis

Blanche's sister Stella is a lot more stable than Blanche. She might not be so bright, which could be why she has settled down with Stanley and reads comics not literature like Blanche. But she is still sensible. For example, she tells Blanche to 'stop this hysterical outburst'. Really, Stella is just an adoring housewife. She clearly loves Stanley and says she has no intention of leaving him – when Blanche says she should after the poker night. Maybe she is even too easy-going, as many women would have left. But she is pregnant, which is a reason not to do so.

Of the two main male characters, Mitch is the more likeable. He is drawn to Blanche at the poker party and shows her his cigarette case, showing he is fairly sensitive. Blanche herself sees that he is not like the other men. It seems for some time that his main fault is being dull. When they go out for the evening in Scene Six, they have had a dull time, but he just makes it duller by talking about his weight. However, he does sympathise with Blanche about her husband. In a way he is practical about their relationship, saying that they both need someone, so why not? But in the fateful Scene Nine we see another side to Mitch. He comes round drunk and in work

A02 Attempts analysis, but lacks explanation

A02 Insightful observation

clothes, and rips off the paper lampshade. This seems almost like an assault on someone so delicate as Blanche. She desperately tries to get him to understand that her behaviour in the Hotel Flamingo was because she was lonely, but he just thinks if she slept with all those men, why not him, and tries to rape her. It is only her calling 'Fire!' that stops him. To be fair, he does try to protest to Stanley at the final poker party, but this is not much use to Blanche.

A02 Simplistic, unless it is referring to melodrama

Stanley, of course, is the villain of the piece. He seems quite pleasant at first, making jokes about alcohol and so on, and asking Blanche about her job, but he soon starts to lose patience with having her there. His first really despicable act is at the end of the poker party, when he smashes the radio and hits Stella – who is pregnant at the time. He is sorry afterwards, but even this could be just a trick. He still shouts for her with 'ear-splitting violence'.

A05 Evidence of interpretation

The next despicable thing he does is to give Blanche a bus ticket to Laurel. This is meant to be a birthday present, so it is especially cruel, as Stella points out. However, his worst crime is obviously when he rapes Blanche in Scene Ten. He tries to make out that it is fate: 'We've had this date with each other from the beginning!' But nothing excuses this kind of behaviour. Even in Scene Eleven he just ignores Blanche, sitting and playing poker like nothing has happened. He is despicable, whereas Blanche shows nobility of character.

A01 Weak conclusion, though it refers back to the question

MID LEVEL

Comment

This response is reasonably well structured, though rather dull in the way it just deals with each character in turn. It does analyse fairly successfully at times, but more explanation is sometimes needed. Sometimes points are unclear, or just drift into retelling. There is only a slight hint of contextual awareness. The conclusion is weak, essentially just agreeing with the statement.

To improve the answer:

Consider disagreeing with the stated view, or at least looking at possible counter-arguments, for a more interesting response. Explain points more clearly and fully, and avoid retelling the story without analysis. Find more ways to address context (AO3), such as 1940s gender values, and consider alternative interpretations (AO5).

Candidate 2

A04 Awareness of genre

In tragedy the hero or heroine has to be basically noble, yet be destroyed by a combination of fate and a personal failing. This seems to be true of Blanche, although she is driven mad rather than dying as in a tragedy like 'Romeo and Juliet'. She is a refined and delicate woman who admits to being 'soft' and to putting on 'the colours of butterfly wings ... to pay for – one night's shelter'. We know that she appreciates literature too. She refers to a story by Edgar Allan Poe and recognises a poem by Elizabeth Barrett Browning. Her sister Stella is also quite refined, but lacks Blanche's appreciation of poetry. Possibly she has played this down in order to live with Stanley. Her reading a comic book in Scene Four shows this. Even Eunice, though a notch or two below the DuBois family, as we can see in her speech, is kind-hearted, as when she welcomes Blanche, and later brings her a gift of grapes.

A02 Effective use of evidence to analyse character

Even though the women are therefore at least partly 'noble' in character, it would be very unbalanced to make the men just 'despicable'. Stanley does some cruel things – the most unforgivable being the rape at the climax. However, some critics, especially in the twentieth century, have justified his behaviour. The director Elia Kazan, for example, did this, and some audience members actually cheered when Stanley carried Blanche off to rape her. Nowadays few critics would go this far. However, Stanley has to be seen in perspective. He is a working-class man in the 1940s who is most at ease in a man's world (like the army). He believes, like Huey Long, that 'Every man is a king'. He says he is 'unrefined', but he resents Blanche's attitude towards him when she calls him an 'ape man' (Scene Four) and later when she and Stella seem to gang up on him, Stella calls him a 'pig', and he smashes the plates. Also, Blanche stays in the Kowalski apartment for around eight months, which must cramp their love life – which is something Stanley values, as does Stella.

A04 Aware of interpretations

A03 Awareness of context

A01 Slightly too informal and needs to explain Blanche's influence on Stella

Mitch seems like a weak version of Stanley at times, but he is a good man in some ways. He is sympathetic to Blanche, realising that she finds it hard being in the apartment during the poker game, though his judgement on Stanley's violence is too mild: 'Poker should not be played in a house with women.' Blanche recognises Mitch's sensitivity, like when he shows her his cigarette case, and when he 'clears his throat', showing his emotion about his mother. We cannot sympathise with him when he will not listen to Blanche when she tries to explain her behaviour at the Hotel Flamingo. However, when he tries to have sex with her, this is really a half-hearted effort, and not quite an attempted rape as some critics claim.

A01 Effective use of evidence

A02 Infers meaning

A05 Personal response to critical interpretation

Blanche is her own worst enemy. She might be a symbol of the defeated South and Stanley of the victorious North. She was so upset by the suicide of her husband that she still hallucinates polka music, and the gunshot. But her behaviour goes beyond just being damaged. For example, we see her flirting with the young man at the end of Scene Five, even though she is about to meet Mitch for a date. It is as if she just cannot help herself, as with the schoolboy who got her fired.

A03 Context, but could be expanded

A01 Valid interpretation, but could be expanded

AO2

Identifies techniques but in a rather hurried way, not quite tied in to the argument

Williams uses different techniques to make us sympathise with Blanche. There is the symbolism of her baths (guilt), her paper lanterns (trying to make magic in her life), and the 'lurid' shapes and jungle noise sound effects in Scenes Ten and Eleven. There is also the the way she often seems helpless, as in her final line in Scene Three, 'I need kindness now' which looks forward to her final line in the play. She ends up a broken woman, lost in a fantasy about dying at sea, then fearfully trying to escape. It could be that she achieves tragic dignity in the final scene, and that the poker players stand up because they recognise this.

AO1

Addresses question

If all the men were just despicable, the play would not be nearly so good. Instead, Williams makes us have sympathy with the men as well as the women. Blanche grows to become dignified, and Stella shows how much she cares about her sister. The women do have the moral high ground, but the men are three-dimensional characters who are products of their time.

AO1

Fairly effective conclusion with final hint of context

GOOD LEVEL

Comment

The candidate responds to the question effectively, showing reasonable awareness of context and critical interpretations. At times points could be expanded or explained more clearly. There is also a tendency to treat the characters as real people, with the recognition of the text as a drama only coming hurriedly in the penultimate paragraph.

To improve the answer:

Explain points and explore ideas more fully – especially context (AO3), and always bear in mind that the text is a drama, with characters who may represent ideas: they are not real people. Interpret techniques in terms of how they create meaning (AO2), rather than listing them. The expression could at times be more fluent.

Candidate 3

A01
Immediately addresses question; strong statement backed by embedded quotes

Williams initially idealises Stanley's masculinity. He is a meat provider who finds 'animal joy' in his existence, and who has 'the power and pride of a richly feathered male bird among hens': he is supremely self-confident, and full of raw energy. Moreover, he gives pleasure as well as taking it. When he meets Blanche he seems friendly and hospitable: 'You going to shack up here? ... Good.' True, he is aware of their social differences: 'I'm afraid I'll strike you as being the unrefined type.' Yet at this point he is not resentful, and it would be misguided to define him simply as 'despicable'.

A03
Topic sentence flags up comparison

Blanche, on the other hand, reveals her faults and weaknesses from the start. We see her snobbish insensitivity when she snubs the lower-class Eunice by curtly rejecting her offers of help and conversation – a snub echoed in Scene Eleven when she rejects Eunice's gift of grapes. This is hardly noble. Left alone, Blanche helps herself to whisky, washing the glass to hide the fact. This reveals her drink problem, her exploitation of hospitality, and her dishonesty. She is insensitively disparaging about the apartment, and patronises Stella ('plump as a little partridge'). Yet she is defensively vain: 'I won't be looked at in this merciless glare!' Admittedly, an alternative view would be to see this as vulnerability, as she is so sensitive about getting older, perhaps because of the obsessive fear of death brought on by her husband's suicide.

A02
Awareness of structure

A04
Aware of alternative interpretations

Stella, by contrast, seems almost saintly at first. She welcomes Blanche, humours her, and puts up with having her home compared with an Edgar Allan Poe horror story. On several occasions she defends Blanche to Stanley, as when he rakes up her past in Laurel, and when he is cruel to her in Scene Eight. Later, though, we will see how Stella's passion for Stanley compromises her morality.

A01
Succinct analysis of language using correct terminology

The characters' flaws become increasingly apparent. In Scene Two, Blanche verbally attacks Stella to forestall criticism: 'I took the blows in my face and my body!' Her melodramatically metaphorical outburst combines manipulation with hysteria. Noticeably she manages to avoid revealing how Belle Reve was 'lost', and the naïve Stella never asks. This is echoed later by the evasive way in which Blanche avoids telling Mitch her age (Scene Six).

A02
Awareness of structure

Stanley is understandably frustrated by his wife's vague acceptance of Belle Reve's loss, and worried that he is being swindled, but we see him in a far worse light in Scene Three. He dictatorially tries to stop the sisters talking, smashes the radio, and then hits his pregnant wife. To most audience members, especially now, this is unforgiveable. Perhaps, if Stella chooses to stay with a violent man, she has only herself to blame. However, she is pregnant by him and, in the social climate of the 1940s, has little choice. Moreover, she enjoys their shared passion. To her, the 'things that happen between a man and a woman in the dark ... make everything else seem – unimportant.'

A03
Context, interpretation

A01
Analysis and personal response

Stanley is perhaps justified in becoming frustrated. Blanche's stay costs him and Stella money and inhibits their lovemaking. Her overheard condemnation of him as an 'ape man' (Scene Four) also fuels his animosity, though his smug confidence in Stella's loyalty, shown by his grinning at Blanche over her shoulder, is chilling.

A05 — Aware of alternative interpretations

However, he plumbs new depths in Scene Eight when he takes cruel delight in giving Blanche the surprise 'birthday remembrance' of a ticket back to Laurel. However, it is his rape of Blanche while Stella is giving birth that puts him completely beyond the pale. His claim that it is fated ('we've had this date …') does nothing to justify it. Later he is 'prodigiously elated' because he has finally beaten Blanche, and got away with rape. One or two critics have taken a similar view to Robin Grove, namely that 'in scene 10, the real unspoken meaning of the play is that [Blanche] really has been asking for what she gets' ('Being Taken for a Ride: A Streetcar Named Desire', 1987). However, this seems unduly harsh. A more convincing view is the 'Darwinist' one – that Stanley simply represents the survival of the fittest, either as an individual or as a representative of a newly assertive working class in the US of the time, tapping into ideas of the American dream. His actions may be despicable, even if his motives are less clear.

A01 — Develops argument

A02 — Interesting argument with correct terminology

Stella may represent the perfect wife, but her passivity is not real virtue. She believes Stanley's story because, as she tells Eunice, she could not live with Stanley and believe Blanche's. She is therefore guilty by default, choosing security and sexual gratification over her sister's sanity. Her rhetorically repeated 'What have I done to my sister?' shows only that she found the choice difficult, not that she regrets it. Her sobbing is just a 'luxurious' self-indulgence, and is therefore hardly noble.

A03 — Context

Mitch is a marginally more acceptable model of masculinity. He is more sensitive than Stanley, as we see when he shows Blanche the inscribed cigarette case 'from a dead girl', and in his love for his mother. However, his clumsy attempt to force himself on Blanche in Scene Nine shows that he fails to understand her vulnerability. He subscribes to the chauvinistic moral double standards of the time when he condemns her as not 'clean enough' to share a house with his mother. His stuttering accusations as Blanche is led away are too little, too late.

A05 — Aware of interpretations and genre; interesting argument

Some critics say that Blanche achieves tragic status, but is this true? Tragic heroism requires the dignity of sanity: hence Shakespeare restores Lear's wits before his death. Blanche, however, remains deluded. She exits calmly only because she is charmed by the courtesy of the only decent man in the play – the Doctor. All four major characters are despicable to some extent – Stanley the most because of his crowing triumph, Stella because of her collusion and betrayal, Mitch because of his double standards, and even Blanche because of her pathetic inability to face reality.

VERY HIGH LEVEL

Comment

An extremely well structured, convincing and fluent response. The candidate shows sound knowledge and uses quotations effectively, and demonstrates real insight, personal interpretation, analysis and alternative critical interpretations. The response also shows awareness of social and literary connections.

PRACTICE TASK

Now it's your turn to work through an exam-style task on *A Streetcar Named Desire.* The key is to:

- Quickly read and decode the task/question
- Briefly plan your points – then add a few more details, such as evidence, or make links between them
- Write your answer

Decode the question

> **'Brutality and betrayal are the triumphant forces at the end of *A Streetcar Named Desire.*'** By considering Williams's dramatic methods, discuss to what extent you agree with this view.

'Brutality'	suggests that Stanley has wilfully and cruelly destroyed Blanche
'betrayal'	suggests that characters have been disloyal to each other – principally Stanley to Stella in raping Blanche, but also Stella to her sister in having her committed, Mitch in failing to understand or defend Blanche, and of course Blanche in prompting her husband to commit suicide
'triumphant forces … end of the play'	suggests that the audience is left with a pessimistic, grim view of human life in which self-interest and cruelty prevail over kindness and loyalty
'dramatic methods'	suggests you must focus on what Williams *does* – not just language, but also structuring of events, and the use of visual and sound effects, and music, for example
'to what extent do you agree?'	what is my view? Do I agree with the statement completely, partially or not at all?

EXAMINER'S TIP

Remember to incorporate the views of critics, but make sure that the central idea is your own. For example, *Director Elia Kazan saw Blanche as a dangerous woman who threatened the Kowalski marriage. Although there may be some truth in this, I think Harold Clurman's view of her as a sensitive victim is far more compelling.*

Plan and write

- Decide your viewpoint
- Plan your points
- Think of key evidence and quotations
- Write your answer

Success criteria

- Show your understanding of the idea of **tragedy** as a genre
- Draw on a range of critical views or different interpretations as appropriate
- Sustain your focus on the twin ideas of 'brutality' and 'betrayal'
- Argue your **point of view** clearly and logically
- Make perceptive points and express your ideas confidently
- Support your points with relevant, well-chosen evidence including quotations
- Use literary terminology accurately and appropriately with reference to the effect on the reader
- Write in fluent, controlled and accurate English

Once you have finished, use the **Mark scheme** on page 111 to evaluate your response.

FURTHER READING

Biographies

Ronald Hayman, *Tennessee Williams: Everyone Else is an Audience*, Yale University Press, New York and London, 1985

A well-written biography with interesting quotations from Tennessee Williams and his friends

Donald Spoto, *The Kindness of Strangers: The Life of Tennessee Williams*, Bodley Head, London, 1985

Crammed with facts yet surprisingly readable

Nancy M. Tischler, *Tennessee Williams: Rebellious Puritan*, The Citadel Press, New York, 1961

A biography focusing on Williams's work

Edwina Dakin Williams, *Remember Me to Tom*, New York, Putnam, 1963; London, Cassell, 1964

Mrs Williams's memories, ghosted by Lucy Freeman. Pedestrian in style but interesting, not least for what Mrs Williams has omitted to mention

Donald Windham, *Tennessee Williams' Letters to Donald Windham, 1940–65*, New York, Holt, Rinehart & Winston, 1977

Of literary as well as personal interest

Literary criticism

Thomas P. Adler, *Tennessee Williams – A Streetcar Named Desire/Cat on a Hot Tin Roof* (Readers' Guides to Essential Criticism) Basingstoke/New York, Palgrave Macmillan, 2013

Reviews critical approaches to the play

Catherine M. Arnott (compiler), *Tennessee Williams on File* (Writers on File Series), London, Methuen, 1985

John S. Bak, 'Criticism On *A Streetcar Named Desire*: A Bibliographic Survey, 1947–2003', *Cercles* 10 (2004)

Reviews and categorises critical approaches

Roger Boxill, *Tennessee Williams* (Macmillan Modern Dramatists), Petersen-Macmillan Verlag, Hamburg, 1987

Follows the standard pattern of modern scholarship: a short biography followed by summaries of the plays

Signi Falk, *Tennessee Williams*, New York, Twayne Publishers, 1962

A discussion of Tennessee Williams's plays, with too much emphasis on summaries of the plots

Philip C. Kolin (ed.), *Confronting Tennessee Williams's A Streetcar Named Desire* (Contributions in Drama and Theatre Studies, No. 50), Westport, CT, Greenwood Press, 1993

Academic contributions of varying value

Richard F. Leavitt (ed.), *The World of Tennessee Williams*, W. H. Allen, London, 1978

A lot of illustrations, some interesting; very little text

Matthew C. Roudané (ed.), *The Cambridge Companion to Tennessee Williams* (Cambridge Companions to Literature), Cambridge, Cambridge University Press, 1997

Academic contributions by several scholars

Nancy M. Tischler, *Student Companion to Tennessee Williams* (Student Companions to Classic Writers), Westport, CT, 2000

Short biography followed by a discussion of the plays

LITERARY TERMS

antagonist character who is the main opposition to the *protagonist*

authorial voice the author, as distinct from the characters he/she has created, speaking directly to the reader

denouement end of the play (or other narrative), in which plot strands are drawn together, questions are answered and conflict is resolved

dialogue lines spoken by the characters to each other

dramatic irony when the audience is aware of key information of which at least one character on stage is unaware

dramatic tension uncertainty of outcome, usually caused by conflict that the audience feels must be somehow resolved; suspense

epigraph quotation placed at the beginning of a poem, novel or play, hinting at its meaning

Expressionist presenting a distorted, exaggerated form of reality. The Expressionist movement started in Germany in the early twentieth century in visual arts, and exercised a considerable influence on drama and film as well as on literature

figurative language language enriched by figures of speech such as metaphor

foreshadow hint at what is to come later in the narrative

genre distinctive type of literature

hubris (Greek) the overweening pride that is the cause of the downfall of a tragic hero

ironic (1) somehow particularly inappropriate, as in the name Elysian Fields for a rundown street; (2) describing comments in which a character says the opposite of what they really mean, as when Stanley says, 'the place has turned into Egypt and you are the Queen of the Nile!' (p. 94)

melodrama play with a sensational plot, a violent, often bloodthirsty incident, and with over-simple characterisation of heroes and villains

metaphor figure of speech in which something is spoken of as if it is something else that it resembles in at least one way, as in referring to sexual desire as a 'streetcar'

morality play a type of medieval or Tudor play with stock characters which aims to educate the audience morally

motif a recurring element that is significant – especially in symbolic terms – in a play or other narrative

pathos quality which evokes strong feelings of pity and sorrow. This quality can of course be tinged with mawkish sentimentality, as in some of Dickens's work

protagonist main character, especially one with whom the reader or audience identifies

rhetoric the use of figurative language techniques, especially to persuade

simile figure of speech using 'like', 'as' or 'than' to compare one thing with another

stage directions text which sets the scene, describes any special effects, and says how the actors should move or speak, as well as pinpointing their entrances and exits

symbolism the use of words to represent something else. The symbolist movement in nineteenth-century literature believed in hidden meanings underlying reality

tableau vivant a living picture, a group of silent motionless actors representing a dramatic event

tragedy play leading towards the death or downfall of a hero or heroine resulting from a **tragic flaw**

tragic flaw traditionally (especially in classical **tragedy**) a weakness in an otherwise noble character that causes their death or downfall

trope any figure of speech in which a word is used to represent something else (a **metaphor** or a **simile** is a trope)

unities the rules demanding unity of time, place and action in a play. These rules came to be ascribed to the Greek critic and philosopher Aristotle, and from the sixteenth to the nineteenth century were regarded by literary theorists as imperative for the construction of a drama

REVISION TASK ANSWERS

Task 1: Character tensions – p. 16, Scene Two

- Stanley suspects, correctly, that Blanche will see him as unrefined.
- Blanche feels that she had to deal with the dying relatives alone.
- Stanley suspects that Blanche has swindled Stella, and therefore him.
- Stella detects something inappropriately flirtatious in Blanche.
- Stella has no interest in finding out how Belle Reve was 'lost'.

Task 2: Stella and Blanche – p. 20, Scene Four

- Stella is dedicated to Stanley and feels real passion for him, missing him desperately when he is away ('I can hardly stand it when he is away for a night' (p. 10)). Blanche seems to have felt a romantic attachment to her young husband, and has engaged in sex with many men to make herself feel alive and wanted, but has perhaps never felt real passion – as opposed to mere desire.
- Stella is outraged by Stanley's violence, but only briefly. That night she makes love to him. She may even find his violence attractive. Blanche finds it appalling – an indication of his brutish nature: 'He acts like an animal' (p. 47).
- Blanche loves literature, especially poetry (e.g. Whitman) and thinks culture is important. She urges Stella not to 'hang back with the brutes' (p. 47). Stella shows no signs of being interested in culture. Instead we see her happily reading a comic book (p. 40).
- Stella has thrown in her lot with Stanley and has no higher aspirations. Blanche associates class with culture, but would probably appreciate more money for the sake of security.
- Stella seems very contented (e.g. p. 40), but Blanche is insecure and unhappy.

Task 3: Blanche and Mitch – p. 25, Scene Six

- Mitch shows Blanche his cigarette case: 'The girl's dead now' (p. 33).
- Blanche appreciates his concern after Stanley's violence: 'I need kindness now' (p. 39).
- Mitch and Blanche go out for an evening. It is dull, but Mitch admits he is fascinated by her: 'I have never known anyone like you' (p. 61).
- She is moved to tell him about her husband. They embrace: 'Sometimes – there's God – so quickly!' (p. 68).

Task 4: Questions for Stanley – p. 28, Scene Eight

- Why are you so anxious to investigate Blanche's past? ('I want to find out the truth because she seems to think she's better than me, and I suspect that she's a lot worse. And I want an excuse to get rid of her.')

- How do you think she regards you, and how do you feel about that? ('I know she thinks I'm an ape man – I overheard her. I resent the fact that she's trying to turn Stella against me.')
- Why did you present her with the bus ticket? ('I want her out of my home – and I wanted to spite her too. She had it coming to her because of the way she looks down on me.')
- What do you think about her morality? ('She acts like she thinks she's a queen, but she's a slut.')
- How is her stay affecting you? ('It's having a bad effect on Stella – making her start to look down on my manners. It also gets in the way of our love-making: we have no privacy any more.')

Task 5: What leads to the rape – p. 34, Scene Ten

- Stanley is friendly and inclined to joke: 'Unless you got somebody hid under the bed' (p. 91). He humours her claims to be going on a cruise.
- He proposes a truce: 'Shall we bury the hatchet and make it a loving-cup?' (p. 92).
- He is insulted by her: 'But I have been foolish – casting my pearls before swine!' (p. 93).
- He changes tack, mocking her claims and her 'Mardi Gras' outfit.
- Feeling threatened, she breaks a bottle to defend herself. He disarms her and carries her off.

Task 6: Responses to Blanche – p. 36, Scene Eleven

- Stella does not know if she was right to have Blanche taken away, but Eunice reassures her.
- Stella does not say much, finding the situation painful, but tries to be kind to Blanche.
- Stanley ignores Blanche. He continues to play cards, 'prodigiously elated', presumably because he has beaten Blanche, got away with rape, and can now get rid of her.
- When Blanche is led away, Stella is emotional ('What have I done to my sister?') but her 'luxurious' sobbing suggests self-indulgence.
- Mitch stutteringly tries to complain to Stanley, and blames him for what has happened to Blanche, but then collapses without offering Blanche real help or solace.

Task 7: Blanche's weaknesses – p. 44, Blanche

- Blanche is vain, though this may be largely due to her fear of growing old, and her even greater fear of dying.
- She is sensitive to slights, but insensitive to her effect on others – hence her criticism of Stella's home and husband.
- She is dishonest, hiding her near-alcoholism and the real reason for her coming to New Orleans.
- She cannot resist flirtation – first with Stanley, and later with the Young Collector.
- She is mentally unbalanced and over-emotional, as in her 'I took the blows' speech (p. 12).

Task 8: Death – p. 54, Death

- Death appears as a theme with Blanche's 'I took the blows' speech (p. 12).
- We also find out, notably in Scene Six, about her husband's suicide, which has left her traumatised and guilt-wracked.
- Blanche and Mitch have death in common – he has lost the girl who gave him the cigarette case, and will soon lose his mother.
- Williams links the themes of death and madness through the use of the polka music and the gunshot, representing death but only heard by Blanche (and the audience).
- Blanche has been unbalanced by her experiences of death at Belle Reve, leading to her promiscuity.

Task 9: How the scenes work together – p. 62, The timeframe

- Scenes One to Six cover the first few days of Blanche's visit; they prepare for the main conflict.

- Scenes Seven to Ten take place within one day in September: the action reaches a climax.
- Scene Eleven is a few weeks later; it shows the consequences and provides a resolution.

Task 10: Contextual influences – p. 70, Historical background

- The play is set in New Orleans, one of the Southern states defeated in the Civil War.
- Blanche and Stella come from an old, once-wealthy and now declining 'plantation' family that made its money from slave labour.
- Homosexuality was illegal when the play was written; Williams was homosexual.
- The Second World War ended three years before the play was first performed.
- Promiscuity was seen as morally shaming in a woman, but not generally in a man – or at least in many parts of society.

PROGRESS CHECK ANSWERS

Part Two: Studying *A Streetcar Named Desire*

Section One: Check your understanding

1. How is Blanche's mental instability indicated in at least one way in Scene One?
- Tells Stella, 'I *can't* be *alone*!'.
- Drinks too much.
- Makes a long hysterical speech about Belle Reve.

2. Write a sentence describing how Stanley responds to Blanche in Scene One.
- He is friendly, mildly curious, and does not seem to mind her staying in the apartment.

3. What is Stella's attitude to the loss of Belle Reve as revealed in Scene Two?
- Stella says, 'Oh, it had to be – sacrificed or something' (p. 17).
- This suggests she is vague about the real cause.
- Perhaps does not care much about it now she is over the initial shock.

4. What is Stanley's attitude to the loss of Belle Reve, as revealed in Scene Two?
- He is suspicious, fearing that Stella may have been swindled.
- As her husband he will lose out by this.

5. How does Mitch explain the violence at the end of Scene Three?
- Says poker should not be played in a house with women.

6. How does the music of Xavier Cugat contribute to Stanley's outburst in Scene Three?
- Blanche and Stella have this music on the radio.
- Stanley objects and throws it out the window.
- Stella complains and he hits her.

7. How does Blanche express her reaction to the events of the poker party in Scene Four?
- Blanche makes a long speech to Stella comparing Stanley and his friends with ape men.

8. What is Stella's attitude to Blanche's condemnation of Stanley?
- Stella tolerates what Blanche says, 'coldly' telling her to 'say it all' (p. 47).

9. How does astrology play a role in Scene Five?
- Blanche guesses Stanley's star sign as Aries ('forceful and dynamic').
- In fact he is a Capricorn (the Goat).
- Ironically, she is Virgo (the Virgin).

10. What does the incident with the Young Collector reveal about Blanche (Scene Five)?
- Shows Blanche cannot resist flirting with a handsome young man, even when the man she hopes to marry is about to arrive.
- Relates to her losing her job for having a relationship with a student.

11. What leads Blanche to tell Mitch about her husband's suicide in Scene Six?
- He says his mother asked her age.
- She responds by asking about his mother.

- She can see that he will miss his mother when she dies.
- This leads to her own account.

12. What question does Blanche avoid answering in Scene Six?
- She avoids revealing her age.

13. What key information does Stanley reveal in Scene Seven?
- Blanche had numerous sexual liaisons in Laurel, especially at the Hotel Flamingo.
- She lost her job because of a relationship with a student.

14. Explain how and why Stanley helps clear the table in Scene Eight.
- He angrily throws plates on the floor.
- This is because Stella calls him a pig and tells him to wash his face and then clear the table.
- He resents her telling him what to do.

15. What reason does Mitch give Blanche in Scene Eight for not wanting to marry her any more?
- He says she is not 'clean enough' to live with his mother – meaning morally.

16. What is the significance of the 'Hotel Tarantula' in Scene Nine?
- Blanche jokes with bitter irony, saying that she stayed at the 'Hotel Tarantula'.
- She is pretending to concur with the likely male view of her as a sexual predator.

17. How and why does Stanley comment on Blanche's appearance in Scene Ten?
- He says: 'Take a look at yourself in that worn-out Mardi Gras outfit, rented for fifty cents from some rag-picker!' (p. 94).
- He is insulting her because she is drunkenly dressing up in what she imagines is the right outfit for a cruise with Shep Huntleigh.
- He wants to destroy her deluded hopes.

18. Sum up three or four key events that lead to the rape in the final moments of Scene Ten.
- Blanche feels threatened by Stanley and breaks a bottle to defend herself.
- He easily makes her drop it, and she falls to the floor.
- He then carries her off.

19. How does Blanche snub Eunice in Scene Eleven?
- Blanche rejects Eunice's present of grapes as probably unwashed, and therefore unsafe.

20. How does the Doctor's behaviour help to preserve Blanche's dignity in Scene Eleven?
- The Doctor treats her courteously.
- He resists the Nurse's proposed use of a straitjacket.

Section Two: Working towards the exam

1. How does Williams reveal the past to be important in the play's plot development?
- Blanche's long hysterical (or melodramatic) speech defending herself on the loss of Belle Reve: 'I took the blows' (p. 12).
- Blanche being sick after telling Stanley 'The boy – the boy died' (p. 15).
- The love letters and family papers in Blanche's trunk (pp. 23–4).
- Stanley's enquiries into Blanche's past in Laurel, and the Hotel Flamingo (Scene Five, p. 51 onwards).
- Blanche confiding the full story of her husband to Mitch (p. 66).

- Stanley telling Stella he has told Mitch about Blanche's past (Scene Seven).

- Mitch telling Blanche he no longer wants to marry her, because of her past (Scene Nine).

2. 'Stella and Stanley's relationship is badly damaged by Blanche's visit.' To what extent do you agree with this point of view?

- Stella and Stanley seem happy in Scene One (when he brings the meat).

- Cracks appear in Scene Two. Stella tells Stanley: 'You have no idea how stupid and horrid you're being!' (p. 19).

- Violent outburst at end of Scene Three could be partly because of tensions caused by Blanche.

- Blanche tries to get Stella to leave Stanley. Stella says, 'I am not in anything I have a desire to get out of' (p. 42).

- Tensions in Scene Eight. Stanley wants to 'get the coloured lights going with nobody's sister behind the curtains to hear us!' (p. 79). Blanche's presence has limited their love life.

- At the end, Stella has had to choose to believe Stanley and not Blanche. She has chosen him, and now has his son, so perhaps their marriage can carry on as before.

3. 'Despite occasional moments of hope, Blanche is essentially doomed.' How far do you agree?

- Blanche is mentally fragile even in Scene One.

- Hallucinated polka music and gunshot (e.g. Scenes 6 and 9) suggest Blanche can never be free of the trauma of her husband's suicide.

- Young Collector episode (end of Scene Five) shows she has a self-destructive tendency.

- Seems hopeful at end of Scene Six ('Sometimes – there's God – so quickly'), but only because she and Mitch both 'need somebody'.

- Mitch and Blanche are completely incompatible, as shown by his complete failure to understand her reasons for her liaisons in Hotel Flamingo.

- Scene Ten shows her response to difficulty is to retreat into fantasy, not deal with it.

- Dramatically speaking, as tragic heroine she is doomed by definition.

4. How does the development of the plot lead us to feel more, or less, sympathetic towards Stanley?

- At first Stanley seems unrefined but friendly.

- Hard to sympathise with him in Scene Three. He is resentful from the start. When Stella and Blanche come home, he resents their talking and playing the radio.

- His throwing the radio out and then hitting Stella is unforgivable – though he seems genuinely needy when he wants his 'baby' back, fearing that she has left him.

- We may feel sympathetic when he overhears Blanche's 'ape man' speech – though perhaps he should confront her about it.

- His enquiries about Blanche seem motivated by spite – though we can sympathise with his desire to get rid of her so that he can be more intimate with Stella.

- His giving Blanche the 'birthday remembrance' of a ticket back to Laurel (p. 80) is cruel.

- The rape is unforgiveable, especially as his wife is giving birth at the time.

5. How does Stella reveal her loyalties towards Blanche and Stanley at various points of the play?

- Stella seems pleased to see Blanche in Scene One.

- Says how she misses Stanley: 'When he's away for a week I nearly go wild!' (p. 10).

- When Blanche tries to get her to leave Stanley, she says, 'I am not in anything I have a desire to get out of' (p. 42).

- Takes Stanley back after his violence in Scene Three and seems happy the next morning.

- Merely listens 'coldly' to Blanche's 'ape man' condemnation of Stanley (Scene Four).

- Accuses Stanley of cruelty to Blanche over the bus ticket (p. 80) and defends Blanche.

- Reveals in Scene Eleven that she has chosen loyalty to Stanley: 'I couldn't believe her story and go on living with Stanley' (p. 99).

Part Three: Characters and themes

Section One: Check your understanding

1. Which characters talk about the 'streetcar of desire', and what does their conversation reveal about them?

- Blanche and Stella (p. 46).

- Blanche is dismissive of 'brutal desire'.

- Stella values desire more and asks 'Haven't you ever ridden on that streetcar?'.

2. Why does Mitch's mother want him to marry?

- She is ill, and wants him to be 'settled down' before she dies (p. 66).

3. Who is the 'gaudy seed-bearer', and how does this description fit the character?

- The 'gaudy seed-bearer' is Stanley.

- He is confident and outgoing in his sexuality, like a cockerel.

- Literally a seed-bearer, as Stella is having his child.

4. Who gives someone a birthday present in the play, what is it, and what does this reveal?

- Stanley gives Blanche a present of a bus ticket back to Laurel.

- This shows he wants her to go and leave him in peace with Stella.

- Pretending it is a present, coupled with his knowledge that she cannot return to Laurel because of her past, is cruel.

5. Complete the line 'You're not clean enough …'. Who says this, when, and why?

- 'You're not clean enough to bring in the house with my mother' (p. 89).

- Mitch says this to Blanche.

- He no longer wants to marry her, because she is morally 'soiled' by her promiscuity.

6. What does Stanley say about his wartime experience, and what does this have to do with another issue raised in the play?

- Stanley says 'Luck is believing you're lucky.'

- He thinks he survived the war because he believed in his luck.

- This relates to the theme of fate, and to the idea of 'survival of the fittest'.

7. Who is described as 'sub-human', by whom, and how does this relate to one or more themes of the play?

- Blanche describes Stanley as 'sub-human', to Stella.

- This relates to desire, as Blanche thinks Stanley is motivated solely by 'brutal desire'.

- One theory is that the play is about Darwinian evolution: the brutal survive.

8. Who mentions the 'Grim Reaper' and how does this relate to another idea in the play?

- Blanche mentions the 'Grim Reaper'.

- This is a personification of death.

- Blanche was worn down by dealing with so many protracted deaths at Belle Reve.

9. Who anticipates dying of eating an unwashed grape, and how does this relate to other aspects of the play?

- Blanche.
- It reflects her snobbishness (social class).
- It shows how she avoids real acknowledgement of death by escaping into a whimsical fantasy about it.

10. How and why does Mitch challenge Stanley at the end of the play?

- Mitch says: 'You … you … you … Brag … brag … bull … bull' (p. 98).
- When Blanche is being led away, he accuses Stanley: 'You done this' (p. 106).
- He 'lunges and strikes at Stanley' (p. 106).
- He blames Stanley for Blanche's breakdown.

Section Two: Working towards the exam

1. Write an assessment of how far Stanley's behaviour throughout the play is justified.

- Stanley and Stella are happy until Blanche comes to stay – though his violence in Scene Three does not seem to be a first.
- His behaviour at end of Scene Three is unjustifiable – unless it can be blamed on poker.
- His enquiring into Blanche's past is partly justified: he resents her view that she is better than him.
- To a working-class man in 1947, Blanche's promiscuity makes her guilty.
- She has lied about losing her job.
- He claims he has to tell Mitch the truth to protect him (p. 74).
- The rape is unforgiveable; the only slight mitigating factors are that Blanche has been flirtatious with Stanley, and that many men at the time would take her promiscuity as an invitation.

2. How do you judge Stella's treatment of Blanche by the end of the play?

- Stella has always been kind and tolerant towards Blanche.
- She has put up with Blanche's criticism of the man she loves.
- She defends Blanche against Stanley's accusations, refusing to believe them.
- She accuses Stanley of cruelty over the bus ticket.
- She says Stanley should not have ruined Blanche's chances with Mitch.
- Her ultimate choosing to believe Stanley's version of events is a betrayal of Blanche.
- She does feel bad: 'What have I done to my sister?' (p. 105).
- Her decision is pragmatic: she now has a child with Stanley.

3. How does Williams explore the theme of death in the play?

- Death is present throughout the play, from the mention of the tram to 'Cemeteries'.
- Blanche's husband's suicide is mentioned, accompanied by the polka music that was playing at the time.
- Blanche's big speech about the dying relatives at Belle Reve (p. 12).
- Blanche is drawn to Mitch because of his cigarette case – from a girl who died.
- Blanche describes the suicide in detail to Mitch in Scene Six.
- The polka music is emphasised in Scenes Nine and Ten.
- Stanley talks about his surviving the war because he believed in his luck (p. 98).

Part Four: Genre, structure and language

Section One: Check your understanding

1. What features make the play a tragedy?

- It has a heroine who is arguably noble.
- She is destroyed (though not killed) by her weakness (her past promiscuity), coupled with fate.
- It could be said that going to the mental institution is a living death.
- There is a sense of tragic inevitability to events.

2. To which of the three 'unities' does the play conform, and what is the effect?

- The unity of place.
- Keeping all the action within (or, for rare moments just outside) the apartment creates claustrophobic tension.
- It highlights the strains on the relationships.

3. In what ways is the play melodramatic?

- The extreme characters of Blanche and Stanley.
- Blanche's descriptions of death, and other references (e.g. Mexican flower seller).
- Violence at the end of Scene Three, and in Scene Eight.
- The suicide of Blanche's husband, because of his homosexuality.
- Blanche's promiscuous past.
- The rape.

4. What is characteristic about most of the scene endings?

- Most scenes end on a dramatic (or melodramatic) action or line, e.g. Scene Six: 'Sometimes – there's God – so quickly!' (p. 68).

5. How can the play be divided into three groups of scenes?

- Scenes One–Six stretch over the first few days of Blanche's visit, in May; they prepare for the main conflict.
- Scenes Seven–Ten take place within one day in September: the conflict reaches a climax.
- Scene Eleven takes place a few weeks later: downbeat resolution.

6. What is unusual about Williams's stage directions?

- They are lengthy and often poetic, as if he intended the play to be read.

7. How is the Varsouviana polka used in the play?

- It is used to evoke the suicide of Blanche's husband.
- Heard only by her, it shows her mental imbalance and sense of guilt.
- Its intensity indicates her mood and increasing instability.

8. Who compares soldiers to 'daisies'? What technique is this? What is the effect?

- Blanche compares soldiers to 'daisies'.
- A simile.
- Suggests Blanche's fanciful nature.
- Suggests that she is growing reckless because she thinks she has lost Mitch anyway.

9. What might Blanche's baths symbolise?

- Blanche's baths symbolise her desire to free herself from her sense of guilt.

- She blames herself because her husband killed himself after she said 'You disgust me' (p. 67).

10. What Expressionistic dramatic technique is used to express the turmoil of Blanche's mind in Scenes Ten and Eleven?

- *'Lurid reflections'* and *'shadows … or a grotesque and menacing form'* (p. 94).

Section Two: Working towards the exam

1. 'Blanche grows to tragic stature during the course of the play.' How far do you agree?
- Blanche is arguably noble, showing an appreciation of poetry, and romantic love.
- Spends much of the play trying to conceal her past.
- Gains our sympathies by showing feeling (and gratitude) towards Mitch in Scene Six.
- She accepts her fate in Scene Nine, risking everything by telling Mitch the truth.
- She seems dignified at the end.
- Her mental instability argues *against* her tragic stature.

2. 'A Streetcar Named Desire is really a melodrama.' How accurate is this comment on the play?
- There are melodramatic elements.
- Extreme characters, sexual guilt, secrecy, violence, dramatic scene endings.
- Visual and sound effects – lurid reflections and jungle noises.
- Characters are too realistic and multi-dimensional for melodrama.
- Stanley is never a simple villain: we can sympathise with him to some extent.
- Blanche is never a simple victim – she does make some choices.
- Stella is not at all melodramatic; play ends with her choice.

3. How does Williams use different sorts of symbolism in the play?
- Stanley brings home meat – traditional masculine provider.
- Symbols of streetcars representing desire and death ('Cemeteries').
- Blanche's baths – her attempt to wash away her guilt.
- Paper lampshade – her efforts to disguise or avoid reality.
- Varsouviana polka music – death of Blanche's husband.
- Poker game – suggesting life itself is a game of chance and bluff.
- Visual and sound effects to symbolise Blanche's mental turmoil.

Part Five: Contexts and interpretations

Section One: Check your understanding

1. What real settings are used in *A Streetcar Named Desire*?
- New Orleans.
  Elysian Fields.
  Desire and Cemeteries are real districts.
  Laurel is a place 200 miles west of New Orleans.

2. How is the American Civil War relevant to the play?
- The American Civil War left the South in economic decline.
- Families like the DuBois got rich from slave labour, but were now in decline.
- Blanche could represent the defeated South.

3. How is the Second World War relevant to the play?
- Second World War only mentioned in Scene Eleven.
- Stanley says he survived because he believed he was lucky.
- His patriotism is partly because he fought for USA.

4. What factors in Williams's personal life find their way into the play?
- Williams was a homosexual, although ambivalent about it.
- He had lived in New Orleans.
- He felt guilty about his sister being institutionalised.
- He was terrified of death.

5. Who directed the first film version of the play, and in what key way does its ending differ from the play?
- Elia Kazan.
- It ends with Stella leaving Stanley.

6. Note down two or three ways in which the play has been criticised in performance.
- John Voight's portrayal of Stanley was criticised as lacking in raw energy and being too civilised.
- A French production was criticised for being immoral – despite France's reputation for sexual tolerance.

7. What play by Chekhov can be compared with *A Streetcar Named Desire*, and how?
- *The Cherry Orchard* is about a declining noble family whose orchard is bought and cut down by an upwardly mobile peasant.

8. List three ways in which *The Duchess of Malfi* is like *A Streetcar Named Desire*.
- Duchess is a widow attracted to a lower-class man (merging Blanche and Stella).
- Her brother is mentally unwell and incestuously attracted to her (cf. Blanche's brother-in-law being attracted to her).
- She is betrayed (as Blanche is by Stella) and murdered.

9. Name one way in which the play might be interpreted according to psychoanalytical theory.
- It might look at the characters as expressions of Williams's psyche, or at the psychology of the characters.
- The play's symbols and imagery would be examples of unconscious impulses at work.
- It would highlight the play's preoccupation with sexual desire and fear of death.
- A Jungian approach might see characters as representing archetypes in the 'collective unconscious'.

10. What might a feminist critique of the play focus on?
- How the play reflects or challenges male-dominated social values.
- It might examine how the text portrays men's moral double standards in relation to women, and women's sympathy, or lack of it, for other women.
- It might investigate female oppression implied in the author's technique.
- It might note that Stanley enjoys women but demands their obedience, whereas Mitch romanticises them.

Section Two: Working towards the exam

1. How does Williams's use of setting contribute to the dramatic force of the play?

- The overall setting of New Orleans creates a relaxed atmosphere in which the marriage of Stella to Stanley is plausible.
- The rundown location shows what Stella has sacrificed.
- It makes Blanche's disapproval possible – a major source of conflict between her and Stanley.
- Apartment is small, making life difficult for the Kowalskis and Blanche.
- Belle Reve and Hotel Flamingo are 'absent settings' that impinge on the action.

2. In what senses is *A Streetcar Named Desire* a play rooted in the 1940s?

- Stanley is an unashamed male chauvinist – the norm at the time.
- Proud of his lack of refinement – reflecting the working man's new status after the war.
- The old values of Belle Reve survive, albeit in decline.
- Stanley and Mitch are typical of the time in condemning Blanche's promiscuity.

3. On what issues might a feminist approach to the play focus?

- Stella's attraction to Stanley's dominance.
- Blanche refusal to be dominated.
- Male attitudes to Blanche's promiscuity.
- Difficulty for an educated woman in finding fitting employment.
- Fact that Stella believes Stanley, not Blanche.
- Blanche's disempowerment in being sent to a mental institution.

MARK SCHEME

Use this page to assess your answer to the **Practice task** provided on page 100.

Look at the elements listed for each Assessment Objective. Examiners will be looking to award the highest grades to the students who meet the majority of these criteria. If you can meet two to three elements from each AO, you are working at a good level, with some room for improvement to a higher level.*

* This mark scheme gives you a broad indication of attainment, but check the specific mark scheme for your paper/task to ensure you know what to focus on.

> **'Brutality and betrayal are the triumphant forces at the end of *A Streetcar Named Desire*.' By considering Williams's dramatic methods, discuss to what extent you agree with this view.**

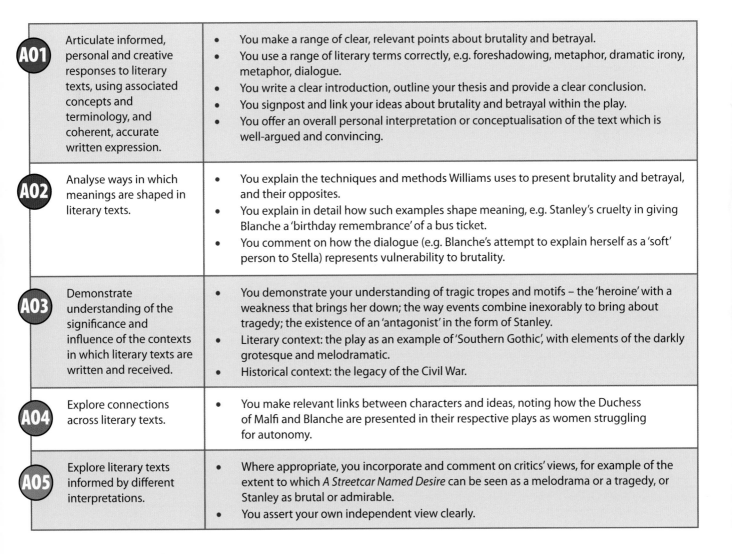

AO1	Articulate informed, personal and creative responses to literary texts, using associated concepts and terminology, and coherent, accurate written expression.	• You make a range of clear, relevant points about brutality and betrayal. • You use a range of literary terms correctly, e.g. foreshadowing, metaphor, dramatic irony, metaphor, dialogue. • You write a clear introduction, outline your thesis and provide a clear conclusion. • You signpost and link your ideas about brutality and betrayal within the play. • You offer an overall personal interpretation or conceptualisation of the text which is well-argued and convincing.
AO2	Analyse ways in which meanings are shaped in literary texts.	• You explain the techniques and methods Williams uses to present brutality and betrayal, and their opposites. • You explain in detail how such examples shape meaning, e.g. Stanley's cruelty in giving Blanche a 'birthday remembrance' of a bus ticket. • You comment on how the dialogue (e.g. Blanche's attempt to explain herself as a 'soft' person to Stella) represents vulnerability to brutality.
AO3	Demonstrate understanding of the significance and influence of the contexts in which literary texts are written and received.	• You demonstrate your understanding of tragic tropes and motifs – the 'heroine' with a weakness that brings her down; the way events combine inexorably to bring about tragedy; the existence of an 'antagonist' in the form of Stanley. • Literary context: the play as an example of 'Southern Gothic', with elements of the darkly grotesque and melodramatic. • Historical context: the legacy of the Civil War.
AO4	Explore connections across literary texts.	• You make relevant links between characters and ideas, noting how the Duchess of Malfi and Blanche are presented in their respective plays as women struggling for autonomy.
AO5	Explore literary texts informed by different interpretations.	• Where appropriate, you incorporate and comment on critics' views, for example of the extent to which *A Streetcar Named Desire* can be seen as a melodrama or a tragedy, or Stanley as brutal or admirable. • You assert your own independent view clearly.